"Thriving in today's workplace takes a lot more than having a specific skill set. True success and happiness lies in an integrative approach to your career. In this book, Mary so beautifully lays out that exact approach. With over twenty years of experience in the corporate world, Mary has taken her years of leadership training, her passion for mindfulness tools, and her love of neuroscience and wrapped into a seven-step process that will give even the most burned out professional a renewed passion back. This is a must read for anyone who wants to love their job again!"

—Dr. Mindy Pelz, Best-Selling Author of
The Reset Factor and *The Menopause Reset*

"Mary and I worked together closely at Cisco and when it comes to combining leadership development, mindfulness and nutrition…I can attest that Mary is the real deal. She not only practices what she preaches, she lives it every single day. Mary offers clients who wish to explore this area a thoughtful, well-researched perspective grounded in real-life practicality."

—Robert Kovach, PhD, Director, Conscious
Leaders & Teams, People & Communities, Cisco

"*Mindful Career* is a complete resource for navigating our careers. With insightful and compelling writing, Mary Mosham creates a clear evidence-based path, chapter by chapter, for bringing our whole selves to the workplace, and ultimately, to life."

—Jennifer Prugh, Founder of Breathe Together Yoga,
Author of *River Offerings*

MINDFUL
CAREER

SEVEN KEYS TO END BURNOUT AND
UNLOCK YOUR GREATEST POTENTIAL

MINDFUL CAREER

SEVEN KEYS TO END BURNOUT AND UNLOCK YOUR GREATEST POTENTIAL

MARY MOSHAM

Editorial work by Eschler Editing
Cover design by MiblArt
Interior print design and layout by Sydnee Hyer
eBook design and layout by Sydnee Hyer
Production services facilitated by Scrivener Books

Published by Mindful Publishing

ISBN: 978-0-578-78594-3

Library of Congress Cataloging-in-Publication Data
Brand and product names are trademarks or registered trademarks of their respective owners.

To my nieces and nephews, may you have the courage to follow your heart's calling and create a career and life that brings you success, happiness, and deep fulfillment. I love you.

Table of Contents

Foreword

Never before have working professionals been challenged to maintain their physical and mental well-being. Over the last decade, work-related stress has increased to unprecedented levels, with nearly 70 percent people experiencing emotional and physical fatigue related to internal and external stressors. This has led to declining job performance, job dissatisfaction, job burnout, and harmful levels of anxiety, isolation, and depression. This problem has exacerbated with the 2020 pandemic. I imagine most of us want the world to return to a level of normalcy, where we can socialize without masks, take our children to school, and enjoy a flourishing economy. When uncertainty prevails, stress and worry escalate. Over time, chronic stress leads to negative physical and mental effects, such as impaired cardiovascular system, elevated blood sugar, poor sleep, and cellular aging.

As a Stanford physician and professor for over thirty years, I have witnessed stress and burnout among my fellow physicians as we manage increasingly demanding schedules, growing administrative duties, and loss of autonomy. We are trained to deliver exceptional quality care to our patients, but not necessarily how to take care of ourselves. Healthcare professionals are not alone with respect to this burnout epidemic. Other professions, including those in the technology field, face this challenge every day. Many people work long hours under high performance pressure, often at the expense of their own well-being.

In her new book, *Mindful Career: Seven Keys to End Burnout and Unlock Your Greatest Potential*, Mary Mosham presents an antidote to stress and burnout. She guides the reader along a path of awakening to one's true authenticity and potential, providing an accessible roadmap to success and happiness. *Mindful Career* offers evidence-based and time-tested tools for curbing burnout, building resilience, and unlocking our potential to maximize the quality of our career and home life during these uncertain times. This book is filled with engaging stories from her leadership journey and other top leaders on how to maintain peak performance without sacrificing what matters most. She reveals her own vulnerabilities with such candor which puts the reader at ease—showing how we are much more alike than different.

Mary brilliantly integrates seven keys to transform personal and professional challenges into courage and wisdom, as well as how to balance our work and life needs to make our unique contribution. This power-packed toolbox will provide a practical step-by-step guide to finding our purpose, building resilience and courage, mastering our negative mindsets, and authentically living our destiny with more success, happiness, and meaning. This is an essential book for busy working professionals to navigate their careers, especially in this fast-paced, changing world.

—Greg Hammer, MD
Professor and Physician of Pediatrics and Anesthesiology
Stanford University School of Medicine
Author of *GAIN without Pain*

INTRODUCTION
The Wake-Up Call

*Life's greatest wake-up calls are an invitation to remember
why we are truly here on this planet and to give space for
something new to emerge that sets our soul on fire.*

We are living in extraordinary and unprecedented times. Over the last decade, the speed and stress of work and life have accelerated at astronomical rates. From growing technology innovations, fluctuating financial markets, looming climate crises to pandemics increasing death rates, we are experiencing more volatility, uncertainty, complexity, and ambiguity (VUCA) across the globe. The term VUCA was based on Warren Bennis and Bur Nanus's leadership theories to help business leaders navigate complex organizational changes and U.S. Army War College students to analyze war conditions after the Cold War.[1]

The constant changes in the global economy and workplace has created a heightened level of uncertainty. It's challenging us to predict the future beyond historical forecasts while responding quickly to changing market conditions. The problems we face are now multi-layered, harder to understand, forcing us to drive decisions and choose the right path forward with limited information. The one-size-fits-all approach no longer works in a VUCA world. We must rely more on clear communication, collaboration across teams, short-term strategic priorities, and the courage and awareness to forge an unchartered path.

These conditions are now a new normal for executives and managers leading their teams and businesses to compete in the global marketplace while navigating their careers. The ability to be flexible, resilient, and to pivot business and marketing strategies rapidly are the new rules of the game, creating a level of stress we have never before experienced. This new world is forcing us to innovate ways to thrive in our careers while we figure out how to work remotely in a digital world, build collaborative relationships across geographies, and solve local and global challenges. Let alone living meaningful and healthy lives.

In this VUCA world, you may feel unyielding pressure. You may be on call 24/7, distracted with endless information, and uncertain how to respond in a world that moves at the speed of light. You may feel overwhelmed, anxious, and burned out with the increasing demands on your career, health, relationships, and finances. You may have lost touch with yourself, the people you care about, and what truly matters. Guess what? You are not alone.

Psychiatrist Edward Hallowell calls this neurological phenomenon attention deficit trait (ADT).[2] ADT is our brain's reaction to the hyperkinetic, external environment of speed, data, ideas, and increased workload and the stress of keeping up with all the demands we face. ADT is different from attention deficit disorder (ADD), which is rooted in genetics and diminishes the brain functions for learning and regulating emotion (especially anger and frustration). Our fast-paced lifestyle requires that our brains track many data points at once—emails, texts, calls, meetings, news, and more—which creates anxiety, hyperactivity, exhaustion, and lack of focus. Unlike computers, which can manage multiple tasks at once—our brains can only manage one task at a time. Many of us think multitasking is a critical skill for being productive; however, researchers claim it has negative mental and physical effects. Consequently, this accelerated speed of life shrinks our brains' functioning, causing more mistakes, stress, anxiety, restlessness, and impatience. Let's explore how Sabrina manages these challenges.

Sabrina's Story

Sabrina was a rising senior leader in a large technology company. She was savvy, smart, and strategic in leading her teams and navigating her career. With optimism and perseverance, she accelerated her career with the best education, top companies, perfect mentors, and the right job roles needed to someday lead a global team as vice president. From multiple promotions, bonuses, and stock grants, she built a comfortable life with her family in the Silicon Valley area. She worked relentlessly to move up the corporate ladder, sometimes even on weekends, to secure her high-paying position and luxurious lifestyle.

On a typical day Sabrina would wake up early, check her smartphone for messages, grab a cup of coffee, and get her kids ready for school. She would then rush to get on the highway and begin the brutal commute to work, sometimes in dead-stop traffic. At work, she was a master of getting things done. She filtered through countless emails, set top priorities, and managed back-to-back meetings with her team and colleagues. At lunch, she ate at her desk while responding to emails or preparing for the next meeting. Breaks to recharge were a luxury. Delivering on promises was her priority. At 6:00 p.m., she drove home through bumper-to-bumper traffic, catching up on the latest news. At night, Sabrina would briefly connect with her family over dinner, then read her kids' favorite books before tucking them into bed. She'd check her smartphone once again and finally crash in bed for the night. The next morning, she'd wake up at the crack of dawn, only to begin the same vicious cycle.

At last, her exceptional performance ratings, savvy leadership style, and unwavering loyalty got her promoted to the director level. She now had more responsibility—a larger scope and bigger team—requiring longer working hours with fewer resources to drive her team charter and business results. Naturally, she approached the situation with the same skills and mindset she used in her last role, only to find herself completely overwhelmed, stressed, and drained by the end of the day. Confronted with imposter syndrome, she felt like a fraud. She doubted her ability to add value and drive business impact. She questioned whether she had made the right choice in taking this larger assignment. The constant organizational changes, managing of team dynamics, and tough conversations with underperforming employees and cross-functional partners were never-ending. Maneuvering corporate politics and juggling multiple competing priorities was taking a toll while her stress and dissatisfaction escalated. Sabrina was finding it increasingly difficult to satisfy her team's and business's needs, let alone her own. She missed the days when she could get things done independently and make a direct impact.

After three months in her new role, the overwhelm and stress turned into unbearable fatigue, anxiety, and other physical symptoms. Coupled with the expanded work scope and health challenges, her mood and positive attitude declined. Sabrina became increasingly impatient and frustrated with her team, boss, and family. The career she's always dreamed of having was crumbling right in front of her eyes—the spark of joy was dying. The leadership role she thought she wanted was killing her soul and impacting her personal relationships. The job that had once given her passion and purpose was now a big thorn in her side, depleting every ounce of her energy. Seriously questioning whether she made the right choice, Sabrina sought my guidance on how to best navigate this new role without driving herself into the ground.

Job Burnout

Sabrina's experience illustrates that a fast-paced, stressful lifestyle is not sustainable and inevitably leads to long-term dissatisfaction and burnout. According to Clokify in 2019, burnout rates in the workplace have increased significantly in recent years, with seven out of ten people experiencing burnout and 50 percent feeling stress.[3] This confirms Gallup's research study of nearly 7,500 full-time U.S. employees showing that 67 percent of them are sometimes, very often or always burned out at work.[4] In severe cases, employees have had mental breakdowns, violent daydreams, sudden resignations, and suicidal thoughts of crashing their cars.

According to the Mayo Clinic, job burnout is a work-related stress, "a state of physical or emotional exhaustion that involves a sense of reduced accomplishment and loss of personal identity."[5] In other words, you lose a sense of who you are because of the exhaustion, creating increased dissatisfaction in your job. Burnout affects your physical, emotional, and mental health and well-being. It also has a huge financial cost to companies. Burnout costs between $125 billion to $190 billion in healthcare costs. Researchers estimate that workplace stress accounts for 8 percent of the national spending on healthcare.[6] Burnout eventually leads to disengaged employees, absenteeism, and employee turnover. Signs of burnout can include:

- increased cynicism, irritability, anger, and impatience with coworkers, customers, or family
- a lack of energy and an inability to be productive and deliver quality work
- reduced satisfaction in your accomplishments
- mental, emotional, and physical isolation and collapse
- sleep disturbances leading to insomnia

- misuse of food, drugs, or alcohol to self-soothe, power through the day, or numb any uncomfortable emotions
- health issues, such as chronic headaches, chest pain, digestive problems, increased high blood pressure and cholesterol, and heart disease and type 2 diabetes.[7]

What causes job burnout? Among the causes listed by the Mayo Clinic are:

- a lack of control and ability to influence decisions with your job
- unclear job expectations and a lack of authority to drive specific business outcomes
- unhealthy workplace dynamics, from coworkers undermining your work to your boss micromanaging or not supporting your success
- a fast and chaotic pace of work that requires you to work overtime, with large scope, and perform without letup
- a lack of social support and feeling isolated at work and in your personal life
- work-life imbalance with too much time and effort on work and less time with family and friends, exercising, and simply relaxing.[8]

We've witnessed this busyness on a global scale with the onset of the 2020 pandemic. In March 2020, the United States and many countries around the world requested a "shelter-in-place" mandate, quarantining people to stay home until the outbreak was under control. The world changed overnight. People wore face masks and practiced social distancing to avoid spreading the highly contagious virus. Schools closed, requiring parents to homeschool. Small businesses closed or pivoted to online platforms and home deliveries, while large corporations requested that their employees work from home. All public events or social gatherings were canceled; only essentials were permitted. In the meantime, financial markets fluctuated and unemployment rates accelerated, perpetuating the fear of a recession in the wake of the pandemic. The world was locked down.

The anxiety, fear, and panic stormed communities. Some people hoarded basic supplies, such as toilet paper, water, and dry foods—while corporations like Cisco, Facebook, Google, and Amazon showed up with tremendous generosity, offering billions of dollars in support of global and local pandemic needs. This global health crisis forced many people to stop the busyness, reevaluate, reset, and realign with what truly mattered. As people turned inward and stayed home, we noticed more kindness and generosity. Families and communities came together. National government and corporate leaders worked together to create solutions. Even the environment benefited from a reduction of pollution in places like China, India, and other metropolitan areas. With every crisis or breakdown, there comes an opportunity for rebirth and renewal. Every failure and setback contain the ingredients to begin again. We rebuild our life from a foundation of what truly brings us happiness, aligned to our authentic being.

If Sabrina's story resonates with you, or if you are experiencing stress or burnout, I want you to know there's an easier way to achieve your career aspirations—a mindful way that supports rather than compromises your health, well-being, and the areas that matter most in your life. Perhaps this health crisis and the constant stress and burnout is a wake-up call to a new way of living and an opportunity for us to live our bigger game. Sometimes we need to change or pivot our careers to allow something new to emerge that supports our well-being and the next level of our growth.

You picked up this book for a reason. Something inside you has been waiting for you to stop the busyness, slow down, breathe, and experience more ease—and joy. Perhaps longing to make a difference in this changing and uncertain world, you've sensed for months or even years that the way you are living, working, and being is not fulfilling your heart's deepest desires. This may have created physical, mental, and emotional distress in your life. You may feel you've been surviving rather than truly thriving. Surviving to maintain your comfortable life-style, your beautiful home, your marriage, or your children's education. Surviving to pay the bills only to discover you've become disconnected from your authentic self. Maybe you've turned to alcohol, drugs, or food to self-soothe or disassociate from your life rather than feel the pain or frustration inside. You may feel a sense of isolation and yearning for human connection. Missing the days you gathered face-to-face with colleagues, family, or friends without worrying about contracting a virus. The high-speed pace may have depleted your focus and resilience—making you less effective in your career. Maybe you've spent your entire life thinking you've created the life you always wanted only to find something is missing—a deep emptiness in your heart.

During the global pandemic, you may have taken action to recharge your energy by starting a yoga practice, meditating, eating healthier, exercising, getting more sleep, and spending more quality time with loved ones. You probably even read self-improvement books and taken online training courses, but still have no idea how to integrate all the information into a practical roadmap. The longing for more joy and meaning in life may have heightened along with the terrifying fear of losing everything you have worked so hard to create. At some level, you may be trying to hold it all together to avoid a breakdown and have no clue how to change your circumstances for the better.

My sincere hope is that this book will inspire you, comfort you, and be your loyal companion as you navigate your career during these uncertain and changing times. Whether you want to explore a new job or career, advance to the next level, reposition your current role, grow your skills, or simply want more work-life balance, this book is for you.

In this book, I reveal insights I learned from over twenty years' experience in corporate management, change consulting, and leadership development in Fortune 100 companies. I will guide you through real-life stories, evidence-based strategies, and research rooted in neuroscience, psychology, physiology, and mindfulness. These pearls of wisdom have empowered me in my career journey as a global leader, in addition to hundreds of managers and executives I've coached around the world.

In our journey together, you will learn seven keys for ending the cycle of burnout and unlocking your greatest potential. These keys are the doorway to your destiny. They are a roadmap to playing your best game at work with not only great success, but with deep fulfillment. You were born with a unique purpose and set of talents designed to help you achieve your dreams and contribute to this ever-changing world. In the third chapter, I will provide an overview of the seven keys and how they work synergistically together. But before we go there, I reveal my personal story of burnout and how a series of wake-up calls catalyzed my growth and led me to my destiny. Let's begin the journey.

MY STORY
The Accident That Saved My Life

At some point, we must let go of the life we planned
and give space for the life awaiting us.

At age twenty-three, I reached a level of financial and personal success I never thought possible. I bought my first home, had a steady
relationship, and was a co-owner in a family catering business. I was on
top of the world, living the American Dream. Two years later, it all came
crashing down. The demands of my career—working weekends and
holidays and being constantly on—had drained my energy. I was overwhelmed with anxiety and depression, which I unconsciously masked
by drinking alcohol to avoid facing the deep pain and suffering inside.
When my five-year relationship sadly ended, I started contemplating a
life change. Although the risks of changing meant leaving everything I
created and severing family loyalties, the risks of staying were significantly worse.

In January 1995, a friend and I drove to Big Bear Mountain in
Southern California to escape the stresses of work and life. As an athlete,
I often turned to competitive sports to work through my stress, and the
ski trip was the perfect medicine. Until the drive home. We took an

alternate route to enjoy the scenic side of the mountain, listening to our favorite music, laughing, and sharing our hopes and dreams. The road was curvy and slightly damp, with ice frozen solid on the embankments. On one of the turns, a boulder tumbled into the middle of the road, which caused me to panic, swerve, lose control of the car, and drive off the icy embankment. As my car tumbled down, I recall my life flashing before my eyes as I repeated uncontrollably "Oh, my God!" Fortunately, we landed upside down in a large tree nestled in a thirty-foot ravine.

There I was, upside down, with no idea how to escape this horrific experience, listening to Elton John's classic "Good-bye, Yellow Brick Road." Mysteriously, I had a burst of adrenaline that allowed me to maneuver my friend and myself out of the damaged car and walk to the main road to flag down another driver for help. Shaken to our core, we were grateful we had worn our seat belts, had minimal injuries, and escaped a catastrophic death. The paramedics arrived immediately and drove us back to the ski lodge. I will never forget the words of one of the paramedics. It still reverberates in my body: "You two are lucky to be alive. The next turn had a 1500-foot drop. You have an important purpose to live."

From tragedy to blessing, this accident forever changed the trajectory of my life. My immense gratitude for being alive gave me the inspiration and courage to make some major changes. I left the family business without regret and invested in a graduate program in organization development at Pepperdine University. With unwavering grit, I let go of a life that no longer served me and began one that was more intrinsically rewarding.

Health and Financial Crises

Thankfully, my life was on track again. I got hired as a learning consultant for a healthcare company delivering training courses to internal employees. Although I loved my job, working and going to school full-time was taking a toll on my body, and my fatigue came roaring back. I knew I had to find other means to manage my stress. My mother's friend suggested I try yoga at a nearby studio. I thought to myself, "what the heck is yoga?" Regardless of my resistance, I was willing to try anything. My physical exhaustion was debilitating.

A typical high achiever, I dove into the yoga practice, taking multiple classes a week and meditating daily. To my surprise, I fell in love with the practice. Within weeks, I felt energized, relaxed, and my fatigue subsided. Inspired, I taught yoga classes to students and faculty in my graduate program. With this renewed energy, I successfully got my master's degree and was ready to conquer the world.

Of course, life had different plans for me. In 2000, after two years of devoted yoga and meditation practice, I had a profound awakening. Integrative medicine expert, Dr. Deepak Chopra, calls this waking up from a dream world shifting from ego consciousness to unity consciousness, where we are connected to a unified field of potentiality.[9] While other teachers describe this transformation as waking up from an unconscious state to an expanded state of awareness beyond our five sensory perceptions. For example, imagine you are sitting in a dark room and you can only see a tiny section of the room. Then someone turns on the light switch and you can now see the entire room, the people in the room as well as your inner world (thoughts, emotions and body sensations)—with crystal clarity. It was like watching the vivid details of a movie on a high-definition monitor. From an outside view, this may sound exciting and adventurous; however, this awakening cracked me open at the core of my being. My entire worldview and my understanding of who I was crumbled before my eyes, leaving me feeling confused yet surprisingly steadfast. My old way of operating in the world radically shifted. I felt connected to something bigger than my human self—an innate intelligence. I became aware of how my thoughts influenced my choices, experiences, health, and relationships. My meditation teacher called this a "rude awakening."

At the same time I was integrating this new awareness, my outer world fell apart. I was laid off from my job and lost my life savings in the dot.com stock-market crash. To make matters worse, I struggled with physical exhaustion again, which I later discovered was chronic fatigue syndrome (an autoimmune disorder). I was living in the VUCA world without any clear understanding or preparation. These compounded life-altering events literally stopped me in my tracks and made me seriously reflect on my karma, choices, beliefs, emotions, and behaviors. I downsized, sold my house, and took a two-year sabbatical to heal my body. I was angry, lost, but hopeful. I remember thinking, "How could this happen after everything I did to change my life for the better?" With relentless drive, I researched and studied. I was determined to find answers and understand the mind, body, and spirit connection. I explored disciplines from spiritual traditions, psychology, physiology to healing modalities. I devoured books, attended conferences and trainings, and finally found a local naturopathic doctor who helped me regain my youthful vitality. During this sabbatical, I pivoted my career, got certified as a professional coach, and began coaching executives through their career journeys.

After two years, I healed my chronic fatigue and was ready for a fresh start. I moved to Northern California to be near the redwoods, capitalize on the growing job market, and be closer to friends. Unfortunately, jobs in the field of learning and organization development were outsourced or only had a small, internal team to lead their people initiatives. There I was, in the midst of recession, with little money and no job. Thankfully, I had my yoga and meditation practice, great support from my friends, and relevant skills to offer a company.

Discouraged about the job market, something inside nudged me to go a local career outplacement center for help. Within a month of attending workshops and searching for jobs, I volunteered my talents as a career coach and workshop facilitator. I was asked to speak in front of hundreds of job seekers about career reinvention and how the recession was the perfect time to find our passion. After my talk, people lined up requesting my guidance. Elated, I set up an office at the outplacement center to support job seekers in finding their next job or career. In that moment, I realized it took losing everything—my money, my job, my health, my identity—to find my purpose and truly be of service to others. My life was not falling apart after all; it was falling together in alignment to my true self. From there, I offered coaching and change-consulting services to local entrepreneurs and finally landed a permanent consulting contract at Cisco Systems. My salary skyrocketed overnight. I managed the change-management activities for Cisco's global partner programs. I loved my job and was grateful to use my talents and make a difference with a team that shared a common mission.

Unfortunately, my healing journey was not over. In 2005, my chronic fatigue syndrome got worse and a tumor the size of a golf ball had developed in my parotid gland. The demands of my consulting job, leading large-scale change projects and traveling to customer sites, was affecting my health and energy levels. As you can imagine, this wake-up call shook me to my core. I was angry and scared yet uncannily resilient. While maintaining my consulting role, I worked with a number of doctors to figure out how to heal my body. I tried holistic treatments, such as juice fasting, liver detoxification, and a four-week holistic-health treatment program, which stabilized my condition temporarily. Over the next year, I finally found an ear, nose, and throat doctor at Cedars

Sinai in Beverly Hills, California, to surgically remove the tumor. It was important to find a doctor who was not only highly skilled but also performed these surgeries weekly versus monthly. I felt blessed to find this experienced and empathic doctor.

In 2007, I had the surgery that saved my life. By this time, the tumor had grown bigger and now engulfed my facial nerve. My doctor and his team removed the tumor after an eight-hour surgery that was originally scheduled for two hours. He later disclosed that my surgery was the toughest case he had ever faced. It required him to tune in to my soul to guide his team not to cut the facial nerve, which would have caused facial paralysis. Unbelievable. I learned in that moment there was a bigger force operating in my life. It was not my time to leave the planet; it was time to wholeheartedly surrender to a higher purpose. Thankfully, the mass was benign and never grew back. From there, I recommitted to a more authentic path of healthy living and selfless service. My faith, family, health, and well-being became my top priorities. I started over—once again.

The Transformation Leader

In 2008, Cisco hired me full-time to lead a global change-management practice for a large, global, cross-functional initiative. The company invested over $200 million in creating a business-to-business ordering management system for customers and partners. Two years into it, the long hours began to take a toll on my body. My stress levels escalated and my health started to decline. Thankfully, with age there is wisdom. I transitioned to another position more aligned to my needs and was hired as a senior manager for a strategic and planning team. In this role, I led a team of change consultants that delivered change and talent management solutions to the business. While I supported senior executives as a trusted advisor for strategic facilitation projects and executive coach for helping leaders advance to the next level. It was a dream job with a creative and talented team. During that time, I expanded my skills, professional network, and acquired certifications in integral coaching and emotional intelligence.

After six incredible years, I reached the top of my game as a change leader and was ready for a new adventure. Unclear about my next path, I spent months contemplating whether I rise through the leadership ranks within a business function or follow my passion in leadership development. Fortuitously, an internal recruiter reached out to me about an exciting opportunity. Cisco's leader development team was looking for a change expert to scale Cisco's coaching practice across the globe. Without hesitation, I accepted the offer. After months of research and piloting a coaching offering, a core team designed the operating model, coaching packages, and trained hundreds of people in a strengths-coaching approach. We democratized coaching to be accessible to all leaders. In 2017, we were thrilled to launch the first global coaching practice in Cisco's history, which now serves over eight thousand leaders with over one hundred coaches worldwide. I was on top of the world. I felt immense gratitude to work for a team transforming the future of work and people development through an innovative strengths-based approach.

After an amazing ten-year career journey at Cisco, I left the company to follow a deeper calling. My gut instincts led me to start my own leadership coaching and mindfulness training business. When we are silent enough to listen to our deepest heart desires, our destiny emerges and illuminates the next step forward. I took a leap of faith and answered the call. Within a month, my business launched, and the stars aligned. The right opportunities and the right partnerships spontaneously emerged. I forged strong partnerships with Cisco, The Marcus Buckingham Company and Potential Project and began coaching leaders and facilitating training programs around the world. These programs focused on leadership and organization development, emotional resilience, and mindfulness training.

For the last two decades, my life has been a series of wake-up calls and career transitions that ultimately led me to this destiny. As I followed the impulses of my heart and inner guidance, I could clearly see how life had prepared me to serve at a whole new level. This was beyond what my practical, logical mind could imagine earlier in my career.

My burnout, discontent, and financial loss had led to breakthroughs, resilience, and a courageous heart to serve others in a broader way. My health breakdowns were the catalysts to help me evolve into a transformational leader and take a stronger stand for my well-being. I aligned with a deeper authenticity and courage and with our planet's natural ecosystem. My definition of success changed. I was less enchanted with rising to the top of the leadership ranks and more motivated by a deeper purpose that served our greater humanity.

The Hero's Journey

My leadership journey is similar to what visionary writer Joseph Campbell outlines about the hero's journey in his classic work, *The Hero with a Thousand Faces*.[10] Essentially, Campbell shares that every hero, protagonist, main character, or leader must, at some point, experience a deep calling to transition to a new career or life. They must undergo a series of trials and tribulations and realizations to evolve, mature, and realize their greatest potential. This is brilliantly depicted in the Star Wars movie series, where Luke leaves his home planet to join Obi-Wan to save the princess and then returns as a Jedi after making peace with his past.

From my most challenging setbacks, I've gained valuable insights that are pivotal to who I am today. It took a car accident, health breakdowns, and financial crisis to force me to slow down and go inward to investigate my beliefs, values, choices, and priorities. Leaving the family business allowed me to forge my own career path and follow a deeper calling. In losing my life savings, I discovered that success is not only about generating financial wealth but about finding meaning and happiness. It's about living in alignment with my authentic self and higher purpose. My health breakdowns made me realize that life is a precious gift. I learned to truly surrender and listen to my inner wisdom and to stay true to my needs, values, and dreams, even when I was unclear about the next steps on my journey. I learned how asking for help was not a sign of weakness but of strength. And I realized that working harder and longer hours was a recipe for burnout and unhappiness—not a badge of honor.

I had to face some hard truths, insecurities, and fears. I lost touch with my essence and with what mattered most. Gratefully, I was resilient and refused to give up, even during my darkest moments. Along the way, I found teachers and mentors who steered me in the right direction. I spent decades studying and doing the deeper inner work, facing my fears and imperfections as well as embracing my uniqueness and innate gifts. I changed my beliefs about work, life, and relationships and let go of ways of working and living that no longer served who I was becoming. I started working smarter, not harder, and living rather than surviving, eventually finding genuine happiness in spite of the setbacks. My health and well-being became my top priorities. I used ancient yoga and mindfulness practices and whole-food nutrition as my refuge and medicine. Being vulnerable and imperfectly human became the doorway to trust, safety, and intimacy in my relationships. And collaborating with others rather than doing it alone was a saving grace. I now coach and train leaders around the world to support them in growing to the next level, cultivating resilience and well-being, and building high performing teams.

The hero's journey is the same journey many of us face in our ascent up the leadership ladder. You may be called to take on broader responsibilities and solve tougher challenges, such as a health or financial crisis, working with fewer resources, or difficult team dynamics. You may be facing your own discontentment, fears, and insecurities and trying to discern how to show up as your best self as a leader without burning out. When leaders take this journey, there's a fundamental, internal shift. They are called upon more often to share their wisdom and lessons learned with their teams, communities, and the broader world.

Life is about the journey, not the destination. You will have setbacks, disappointments, and failures in your career. And, you will have breakthroughs, joys, and successes. But success is not measured by the number of times you fail; it's measured by the number of times you have the courage to persevere and start again. It's about trusting the process of your destiny unfolding and knowing that something beyond your human existence is operating in your life. In crisis lies opportunity and growth. And in growth lies the key to your greatest potential.

This book further unpacks the learnings of my career journey and gives you practical, evidence-based strategies and tools that will help you thrive and grow to the next level. In the next chapter, I reveal the seven keys for ending burnout and unlocking your greatest potential—a life you have been preparing for since you were born. This book is the map to your hero's journey. It's designed to help you build resilience and play your best game at work and in life.

OVERVIEW
The Seven Keys Revealed

Adversity is the greatest teacher for our evolution and maturity to live our unique purpose with passion—fueled by the drum beat of our soul.

One of the world's greatest innovators, Steve Jobs, was known for his visionary and charismatic leadership and transforming the personal-computer industry. Adopted and raised by middle-class parents in Silicon Valley, Jobs was deeply passionate about engineering and spiritual development; he even made a pilgrimage in India to learn Buddhism. In his twenties, he dropped out of Portland Reed College, got a job as a video designer for Atari Corporation, and later teamed up with his friend Stephen Wozniak to start up Apple Computer Corporation. By the 1980s, after two releases of the Apple computer, the company was seeing record-setting public stock offerings. Jobs hired PepsiCo's John Sculley to run the company as their CEO, which eventually led to his resignation due to their conflicting management styles.

Following a deeper calling, Jobs launched NeXT, a hugely successful computer company known for its powerful workstation computers using the NEXTSTEP innovative software system for the education industry.

By 1996, Apple had suffered huge financial losses and was on the verge of collapse. Gilbert Amelio was hired as Apple's new CEO. Fortuitously, Gilbert bought NeXT for $400 million, and Jobs returned to Apple as a consultant. When Jobs returned, innovation and sales exploded. From 1997 to 2007, his team expanded Apple's personal-computer business to the music and telecommunications industries, creating incomparable products, such as the iMac, Mac laptop, iTunes, and iPhone. These innovations reinvented Apple, and Jobs took over as CEO. Unfortunately, in 2003, Jobs had a health crisis and was diagnosed with a rare form of pancreatic cancer. He resigned as CEO and died in March 2011, leaving a powerful legacy that forever changed the world.[11]

Jobs's leadership story is an example of the hero's journey and a leader following his destiny. The universe often presents us with gifts and opportunities that initially look like roadblocks. When this happens, it's how we respond that determines the course of our career journey. Jobs could have let his "failure" at Apple dictate the rest of his career, but he chose instead to face the challenge of reinventing his career. Being forced to resign from Apple was the best outcome for Jobs as it allowed him to learn and create innovative software technology to later share with Apple, which revolutionized the personal computer, music, and telecommunications industries. Although his career path was not a direct path to success and he experienced many setbacks, including near bankruptcy, he persevered and trusted the drumbeat of his soul. He found the courage to be authentically himself, especially during the early years of his career, with his casual attire and long hair, unconventional style, and strict fruitarian diet. Being comfortable and confident in his skin was what made him a unique and powerful innovator and leader.

Jobs's story illustrates the unwavering commitment it takes to follow a deeper calling. He writes: "Have the courage to follow your heart and intuition. They somehow already know what you truly want to become." With the seven keys, you will learn the science, research, wisdom, and best practices behind my personal journey and the journeys of other high-performing leaders. The trials and tribulations of life are essential in unlocking our infinite potential, cultivating mastery in our vocations, and building the physical, mental, emotional, and intuitive capacities that allow us to be our most powerful and authentic selves.

This vertical approach to human development is contrary to traditional development methods. We often think of development as building knowledge and skills to be successful in our careers. However, over the last two decades, researchers illustrate we are only scratching the surface in accessing our full intelligence. They have discovered we have three brains—head, heart, and gut. Each of these brains has their own neural networks that gathers, processes, stores, and acts upon information. They are designed to help us grow, adapt, and react to internal and external stressors or our environment. Although we spend much time focusing on the mind, the gut and heart play an integral role in learning and growing our innate intelligence.

Gallup research shows only 35 percent of people are highly engaged at work in the USA while 65 percent are actively disengaged at work.[12] This is compelling evidence that our traditional methods of engaging people are not working in this dynamic, VUCA world. People, especially millennials, will leave companies if they are not energized, engaged, and happy at work. We have a big opportunity to expand our levels of intelligence for the sake of our careers, lives, children, and world. This book is a starting place.

The seven keys provide a comprehensive guide for growing your body, head, and heart intelligences and building resilience (the ability to quickly adapt and recover from stress, setbacks, and challenges). They are intentionally outlined sequentially to help you cultivate the capacities and mindsets to be more engaged and joyful at work and in life. Think of them as a software upgrade to your internal operating system. To move to the next level of your career and fearlessly travel your destined path, you may need to uninstall old software files or beliefs no longer serving your highest good.

The Seven Keys at a Glance

The first key on the journey is to *Find Your True North*. This key is foundational to helping you discover what truly makes you come alive. It's designed to help you get clear on your life purpose, unique strengths, "zone of genius," and core values—igniting the passion and motivation to navigate your career. You will discover the art of crafting an inspiring vision and clarifying the skills and expertise you need to live your purpose with confidence and mastery. I will reveal the Life Compass Map to assess where you are today and where you want to be in the future to make your vision a reality.

The second key is to *Put Your Oxygen Mask On First*. In this chapter, you will gain best practices in self-care and time management to reset, recharge, and recreate a sustainable way of working to avoid burnout. Though this is a crucial step on the journey, it's often overlooked due to the busyness of our work lives. I will uncover the misconceptions and obstacles that get in the way of you taking care of yourself. In addition, I will outline key strategies to help you stay resilient, productive, and joyful to support your team, company, family, and community.

The third key is *Recharge and Nourish Your Body*. Our fast-paced lifestyles take a toll on our bodies, leaving us feeling exhausted, disengaged, and unhappy. I will guide you on how to restore, nourish, and strengthen your body to revitalize your energy and well-being. We review the science behind stress, explore the language of our body's intelligence, and learn how to end the cycle of burnout. You will receive a checklist on how to transform your sleep habits to experience more restful sleep. We will explore how mind-body practices, such as yoga and qigong, strengthen your nervous system and cultivate a sense of calm, clarity, and vitality. You will learn why nature is the new medicine for regulating stress and strengthening your nervous, immune, and other body systems. Lastly, we will uncover cardio exercises and nutrition guidelines to keep you fit, healthy, strong, and performing at your best.

The next three keys take you on a deeper inner journey, where you'll discover how to cultivate greater mental, emotional, and intuitive capacities to navigate your career journey with more confidence, equanimity, and resilience. The fourth key, *Master the Monkey Mind*, will uncover how to shift negative mindsets to positive mindsets and unlock your innate intelligence. You will learn the meaning of a monkey mind and the science and research behind why it's difficult to stay focused, calm, and present in this digital and ever-changing VUCA world. I will introduce you to mindfulness strategies to cultivate more relaxation, creativity, and resilience to stay committed to your career, especially when you are ready to give up.

The fifth key, *Grow a Resilient and Courageous Heart*, will reveal the emotional side of burnout as well as how to build an emotional resilient and courageous heart for handling stressful situations. You will learn emotional intelligence skills and heart strengths to better adapt to adversity and enhance your relationship with yourself and others. The sixth key, *Be Your Authentic Self*, will show you how to surrender and listen to your intuitive guidance and be bravely vulnerable. You will learn how to amplify your authentic voice and unique strengths with unshakeable confidence.

The final key, *Create Your Roadmap to Success and Happiness*, integrates everything you have gathered from the previous chapters. It guides you in creating a roadmap with clear goals and actions to keep you focused and motivated to achieve your True North. Next, we explore how to courageously navigate potential roadblocks along the path. You will learn when to pivot your roadmap in times of change and uncertainty and how to build a network of supporters—those who champion you along your journey to achieve your dreams. Finally, we conclude by revealing the purpose of the seven keys and how to authentically live your life with no regrets. These keys become your toolbox for personal resilience as you make a unique difference in the world with more success and happiness.

This book is designed to help you investigate your inner world—your dreams, thoughts, emotions, and body sensations—and walk away with practical tools you can apply right away. To get the most from this book, find a quiet space and grab a notepad or electronic device. Explore the exercises and reflection questions and experiment with the practices most relevant to your personal needs. There are no right or wrong answers. Give yourself permission to contemplate the questions, explore your inner world, and trust your inner guidance will lead you to the next step. Science shows that writing our thoughts down (especially manual writing) declutters the mind. It helps us retain what we've learned and to grow positive mindsets and habits as we strive to achieve our goals. Now, it's time for you to find your True North.

KEY #1
Find Your True North

*The secret to finding your purpose is understanding what makes
you come alive. When you bravely share your unique strengths and
talents, you liberate others to do the same.*

In my late twenties, I was a learning consultant for a healthcare company delivering professional development workshops to internal
employees. My boss nominated me to get certified in Franklin-Covey's
project-management course—a five-day train-the-trainer workshop
in Utah, USA. Throughout the training, I was bored, disengaged
and counting the hours until the training was over. Mostly, because I
didn't understand the technical jargon nor find the content interesting.
However, on the last day, my energy shifted. The instructor asked the
students to summarize what they learned on a long roll of butcher paper.
Afraid I might appear stupid in front of my peers, I sprung from my
chair, grabbed some colored markers, and started writing. Surprisingly,
a burst of inspiration came as I synthesized the project-management
concepts in a creative, graphic design. The creative energy was potent
and powerful. I felt unstoppable. I ended up capturing the entire process on that butcher paper. The instructor was smiling in appreciation.
I returned to my chair full of energy, actively engaging with the other
students. Something inside me woke up. It was the first time I felt alive
in my job. I was amazed how fast I shifted from complete boredom

to full engagement. That week was a game changer for my career. From that point on, I pursued only work that gave me energy and passion and stopped accepting assignments that depleted my energy. That year, I enrolled in a graduate degree in organization development, where I studied individual and organization transformation and adult learning methods. This eventually launched my twenty-year corporate career in leading large-scale change and pioneering leadership development programs.

What Makes You Feel Alive?

The first key on your journey is *Finding Your True North* or clarifying what makes you come alive. We saw this in Steve Jobs's leadership journey. He dropped out of Reed College to start up Apple Computer. Then, after he was forced out of Apple, he launched NeXT and eventually came back to Apple as the CEO again. By staying true and listening to his instincts, he ended up leaving a legacy that revolutionized the personal computer, telecommunications, and music industries. Who would have imagined the iPhone would allow us to email, text, call, watch videos, take pictures, and connect around the world? When we listen to our internal nudges, or instinctual biological drivers, we naturally become drawn to certain work, activities, and experiences. These natural instincts lead us to what I call our "zone of genius" and, ultimately, our life purpose.

Throughout my life, there have been magical moments when I felt this creative energy. In school, I was energized by creative writing; public speaking; coaching my classmates; analyzing complex math problems; engaging in sports; debating psychological, social, or philosophical issues; and designing learning experiences. In my career, I loved activities that made a difference in people's careers, such as building change management and coaching practices, coaching leaders to build great careers and teams, and teaching seminars. I had this innate ability to synthesize complex information into simple models to support adult learning, build consulting practices, and innovate new solutions. Like a musician composing a symphony or an artist creating something amazing on a canvas, streams of inspiration would come through me. We all have innate gifts. It takes self-discovery, learning, and practice to amplify them in our jobs.

In a 2018 Gallup study, researchers analyzed 230 different engagement studies to determine how well employee engagement predicts key performance outcomes. These studies spanned 230 organizations in 49 industries and 73 countries, covering 1.8 million employees, or 82,000 teams. The business results were astounding. The research confirmed that when teams played to their strengths, employee engagement and business performance increased. They found a 10 percent increase in customer satisfaction, a 17 percent increase in productivity, a 21 percent increase in profitability, a 24 percent reduction in turnover, and a 41 percent reduction in absenteeism.[13]

How do you discover your strengths? Talent-development expert Marcus Buckingham defines your strengths as "an activity that makes you feel strong."[14] Traditionally, corporations have defined strengths as tasks or actions you perform well at doing. These include knowledge, skills, and talents. However, excelling in today's talent market requires more than having the right skills. It requires energy and passion to spark motivation. When we participate in activities that give us energy and passion, we grow exponentially, perform at peak levels, and find deeper fulfillment. To discover your strengths, revisit your education and career journey and notice which activities you naturally gravitated to and which ones you resisted. Were you the person who loved presenting in front of the class, debating a particular issue, writing summaries of classic novels, performing in theater productions, engaging in team sports, analyzing mathematical algorithms, or solving complex problems?

When we investigate our strengths, we begin to understand our zone of genius. These strengths are instinctual and inspire us to show up as our best selves at work. When we lead from our unique strengths, people naturally gravitate to us and our jobs no longer feel like a huge burden. Success and happiness naturally flow because we are doing what we love rather than what we loathe. Take some time to reflect on the activities you are good at and that energize you, and see how you can amplify those activities at work. These strengths can include creating marketing campaigns, presenting at a conference, building a vision and strategy, writing software code, designing innovative products to sell in the market, developing people, building teams, or closing sales deals.

Although strengths are a strategic lever to increase business performance, less than 20 percent of those in the workplace use their strengths in their jobs on a daily basis. Most people are working in jobs that are unfulfilling, unengaging, and that drain their energy. This can ultimately lead to burnout. Marcus Buckingham calls this type of activity our weakness. We often believe we need to focus our energy on our weaknesses to become a well-rounded leader or individual contributor in our careers. But based on their research in *Nine Lies about Work*, Buckingham and coauthor Ashley Goodall assert that developing well-rounded individuals is an ineffective strategy for increasing performance.[15] Instead, it's about amplifying and growing an individual's unique strengths. It's focusing on and developing people's strengths that will help you and your teams thrive. Jobs's relentless drive for innovation helped him lead Apple to global success, and Martin Luther King, Jr.'s passionate dedication to nonviolence helped change hearts and minds during the Civil Rights Movement.

Since it's often difficult to have a role that plays to your strengths 100 percent of the time in the workplace, here are three proven strategies for managing your weaknesses to help maintain your peak performance. First, stop or minimize the activities draining your energy. There are activities that can be streamlined or dropped altogether because they don't add value. For example, you may have a project that is no longer relevant to the current strategic direction or marketplace. This is a perfect opportunity to influence your manager to deprioritize this project from your work scope and repurpose your time for work that fuels your energy and passion. Second, delegate to a team member, or partner with another coworker who loves that type of activity. One great advantage about being on a team is that you benefit from each other's complementary strengths. Your weaknesses can be another person's strengths. By partnering with another person, you create a win-win solution. Finally, reframe the activity in a way that evokes inspiration. In designing a global coaching practice for Cisco, I resisted doing the financial-modeling projections. When I focused on why it was important to get funding, to help thousands of leaders to get coaching, and to support the company's success, I felt inspired and became reengaged. Take some time to think about those activities that weaken you and see how you can reduce them at work. These weaknesses can include detailed administrative work, program or project management, negotiating deals with customers, presenting to groups, researching, managing office politics, or creating marketing content.

Megan's Story

Megan was a product-marketing manager at a technology company. She was creative, ambitious, deliberate, and ready to make an impact on her career. Unfortunately, Megan's job was not maximizing her strengths, and her team was experiencing major organizational and leadership changes that were dramatically shifting the team's charter. Feeling undervalued, discouraged, and demotivated with her project assignments, Megan was ready to explore how to transform her career experience and be inspired by a meaningful purpose. During our coaching engagement, we explored whether she should stay in her current role or find another role within the company that better aligned with her strengths and career goals. Of course, we started with the questions "What makes you feel alive?" and "What is your True North?" Then we examined her strengths, weaknesses, values, concerns, and career interests.

During her self-discovery, she realized she loathed creating content for short-term marketing campaigns but loved researching, strategizing, and leading marketing campaigns that enhanced customer experience. Megan finally understood why her current role was draining her energy. She was spending most of her time doing things she loathed and resisted and less of her time on the things she loved and gave her energy. Although nervous about losing her job, Megan finally mustered the courage to talk to her manager. Surprisingly, her manager was supportive and repurposed her role to play to her strengths. Two months later, Megan was researching industry trends and presenting compelling campaign stories that helped internal stakeholders leverage her marketing programs. She was adding value to her customers and feeling happier and more confident in her job.

Values

Values are the concepts or principles that we consider to be good, important, and valuable in our lives and careers. They help us to create the life we want to experience. Everyone's values are different. Some value intrinsic and intangible rewards, such as love, recognition, intelligence, integrity, generosity, and respect. Others value more extrinsic or tangible rewards, like travel, wealth, work-life balance, flexibility, and autonomy. As children, we may have adopted the values our parents and teachers believed were important for us. However, as adults, it's a good idea for us to determine for ourselves what we value most.

There are many benefits to getting crystal clear on your core values. First, values help you find your purpose. When you understand what is important to you, you have a better understanding of what you want from life. Second, values guide our behaviors. They help us know how to respond to a difficult situation with clear-minded decisions rather than reacting emotionally or driving our own agenda. By clarifying what we want and what is important, we can more easily let go of the things that waste our time and energy. Third, our values become our compass for choosing the best career path. For example, if you value variety, travel, wealth, and interacting with people, a job that requires frequent travel and meeting customers on location may be perfect for you. Knowing your values will determine whether leading a team or being an individual contributor is the right path. Next, when we are clear about what we want, we naturally feel more safe, stable, and confident. We rely less on the approval of others and more on internal validation. When we are in the right career, we feel more purposeful, powerful, and confident in handling difficult situations, making decisions, and adding value to the company. We experience more growth and success as well as fulfillment.

Values Exercise

Make a list of your core values—those things you deem essential for finding fulfillment in your job. These can include things like integrity, autonomy, making a difference, generosity, recognition, flexibility, life balance, creativity, collaboration, teamwork, leadership, spirituality, and freedom. Brainstorm your own list of values, narrow down the list to the top ten, and rank them in importance. From that list, which values are missing in your career? How might you better incorporate more of those values in your life? This is important to remember as we explore crafting your purpose, vision, and roadmap. However, since values change and evolve as we grow, hold them lightly.

Purpose

Now that you understand your strengths, weaknesses, and core values, let's clarify your life purpose. Neurologist, psychiatrist, and Holocaust survivor Viktor Frankl devoted his life to studying and understanding meaning. In his famous book, *Man's Search for Meaning*, he shares how he heroically survived the Holocaust in World War II by finding personal meaning in the experience and helping others survive, even while losing his wife and children. He writes: "Everything can be taken from a man but one thing: the last of the human freedoms—to choose one's attitude in any given set of circumstances, to choose one's own way."[16] One reason he survived the concentration camps was his commitment to completing his book before he died. In this book, he later established a well-known therapeutic method called logotherapy, which helps people uncover their sense of purpose, especially during suffering and existential crises.

Having a purpose, or True North, gives us direction in our career and life. Early in my career, I never contemplated what brought me meaning and purpose or the legacy I wanted to leave when I left the planet. I was more enamored with living the American dream, traveling, and doing the things I loved without having to worry about money. This mindset, of course, led to tremendous burnout, illness, lack of meaning, and unhappiness.

Many successful CEOs exhibit an infectious passion and unwavering commitment to their purpose, or mission. Dr. Zach Bush is a triple board-certified physician in internal medicine, endocrinology, and metabolism. His passion centers around changing the food-production and medical industry through regenerative farming and breakthrough science to deliver, with his team, new insights into human health and longevity. CEO of Facebook, Mark Zuckerberg's mission is to "give people the power to build community and bring the world closer together."[17] While Tesla CEO Elon Musk's mission is to accelerate the world's transition to sustainable energy with electric vehicles that perform exceptionally while reducing our planet's carbon footprint. Each of these visionary leaders are driven by a powerful mission that transforms and benefits our world, planet and future generations.

We all have a unique purpose. It's encoded in the depths of our souls. Sometimes the stars align, and we are led to a sudden realization of this purpose. Sometimes it takes our entire life to find our purpose. But rather than wait for the perfect circumstances, consider spending some time contemplating these two questions: "Why am I here on this planet?" and "What unique gifts and contributions can I give to the world?" Examining our strengths and reviewing the specific life experiences where we are most joyful, alive, and fulfilled is a great way to start. When coaching clients, I often ask, "What do you want to be known for, or what do you want others to share during your eulogy?" These questions help crystalize what is truly important. When our lives align to a higher purpose, we align to a greater source of authentic power and inspiration. We become magnetic and have more access to our inherent intelligence and personal power. People will be drawn to your energy and inspired by your authentic leadership style. We were born to shine and share our innate talents at work rather than hold back and settle for work with no meaning or significance. When we discover our purpose, we are naturally guided on the next steps on our career journey. Here are five simple steps to craft your life purpose statement and align to your True North. You'll know you landed on your purpose when you experience a strong visceral resonance in your body.

1.   Write down three to five events in your career or life where you felt joy, aliveness, and passion.
2.   Identify your top-five strengths or zones of genius.

3. Clarify what impact or outcome you want to have on others or our world.

4. Clarify why it's important to you.

5. Put it together into a single statement using this template: "My purpose in life is to use (top two or three strengths) to impact (who) because (why is this important)."

Vision

Where do you see your career five to ten years from now? In Michelle Obama's book, *Becoming*, she shares about her childhood roots as an African American, her experience as a mother and former United States First Lady, and how her life obstacles shaped her in becoming the influential woman leader she is today. She further shares how she did not expect Barack Obama to become the United States president, though it ultimately gave her the platform to lead some powerful initiatives in public health, human rights, and education.

In today's VUCA world, it can be extremely difficult to predict where you will be five to ten years from now since the way we do business and the workplace may dramatically change. Having a vision for your career and life is helpful in navigating uncertainty and keeping you focused on what matters most. Having a vision inspires you to reach a new level of growth and success you never imagined. A vision helps you fall in love with a dream or idea of a better future.

To create a vision, start with the end in mind. For example, at twenty-six, I envisioned being a consultant who helped leaders grow their careers and skills, build great teams, and foster a culture that inspired people to grow their potential. I also saw myself involved in social change, helping children who were less fortunate. By my forties, I was living my vision as an executive coach and expert in the field of leadership, mindfulness, and transformation. I also became a sponsor for Tibetan children refugees, providing education services to help them realize their dreams. When I first pictured this future, I certainly did not know how to achieve my vision. My path was certainly not clear, but something deep inside my heart, the drumbeat of my soul, led me in the right direction.

Another way to craft a career vision is to understand the discrepancy between where you are today and where you want to be in the future. Motivational psychologist Gabriele Oettingen calls a variation of this strategy "mental contrasting," which means supplementing your vision with potential obstacles and the specific actions you'll need to move forward for a more realistic picture.[18]

Research suggests that change happens when we recognize the gap between our current self and future self. A career vision requires not only a detailed picture of where we want to be in the future but also a detailed picture of where we are today. Mental imagery, or visualization, is a practice that is as important as physical training for athletes.

At eight years old, Michael Phelps wrote, "I want to make it to the Olympics." By fifteen, he won his first gold medal, being the youngest male athlete to set a world record in swimming. But his vision didn't stop there. Twenty-eight Olympic medals later, Phelps visualizes the perfect race every night before he goes to sleep—including the tiny details, like water dripping from his face and his ideal race times. Phelps doesn't just have a vision for his ideal career. He had a vision for each aspect of the race to achieve his goal.

Life-Vision Exercise

Take a moment to quiet your mind and visualize where you want to be five and ten years from now. Gently close your eyes, root your feet on the ground, and turn inward. Relax your body, neck, shoulders, and arms to the best of your ability. Scan your body for any tension or tightness with every inhale and relax and release any tension with every exhale. Keeping your breath as your anchor, in a nonengaging and neutral way, observe any sensations, emotions, and thoughts as they arise. When your mind wanders from your breath, relax your body, let go of the distraction, and return your focus to your breath until your mind is steady, spacious, and still. Now imagine your career and life ten years from now and, without judgment, notice what images or ideas flash in your awareness. Listen intently, as if someone were going to tell you a secret. Perhaps you see yourself speaking on stage, leading a team or business, starting a company, getting married, having a family, living in the city or suburbs, writing a book, or living in another country.

With that image in your mind, feel and sense what it's like being your future self. Do you feel excited, expanded, happy, and fulfilled? What strengths do you already have to realize this vision? Get into the details of your vision. As ideas begin to arise, write them down. If you don't get a clear vision or any ideas, do not worry. You can continue inquiring and reflecting on what's important for you to experience and become in this life. Allow something to arise naturally throughout the week. When we engage with our imagination, we often get inspiration while doing nonconceptual activities, such as walking, hiking, washing the dishes, or taking a shower. These activities engage our five senses and unplug us from our conceptual thinking mind. It's not about rushing the process. It's about trusting the process. It's about knowing, deep inside your heart, you have an important destiny to live that is uniquely designed for you. Positive visions are a powerful force. They energize us with the courage and passion to accomplish our dreams with unwavering commitment.

Skill Development

Now that you understand your strengths, values, purpose, and vision, let's talk about the role of professional skill development in helping you build mastery and confidence. Think about what skills you already have and what skills you'll need to reach your vision. These skills are most likely a constellation of your core strengths, such as strategic planning, program management, public speaking, verbal and written communications, product management, coaching, software engineering, and executive presence.

With every career transition in my life, I clarified what skills, training, experience, or certifications I needed to be hired for my next role. I often worked with a coach and took on a stretch assignment in my current role to gain the experience and confidence needed to expand my skills or reposition my personal brand. Sometimes it can be challenging to reinvent your brand after working in a company for a long time. Sharpening your skills and experience builds credibility and makes the transition to another role easier. Take inventory of your current skills and decide where you want to be five years from now. In Key #6, you will learn how to formulate a brand statement, while in Key #7, you will translate your skill development needs into specific goals and actions.

Life Compass Map

Another important factor in finding your True North is finding the right balance between creating a thriving career and living a meaningful life. To make this easy, I created a Life Compass Map to help you assess where you are today and where you want to be across the ten key life areas shown in table 4.1.

In the center of the model is our well-being. Well-being is the union of health, happiness, and prosperity. "It includes having good mental health, high life satisfaction, a sense of meaning and purpose, and ability to manage stress."[19] This inner circle is comprised of four distinct areas of well-being: physical, mental, emotional, and spiritual. Our physical well-being includes our overall physical health as related to lifestyle and diet, cardio exercise, mind-body awareness practices (such as yoga and qigong), and optimal energy levels. Our mental well-being involves our cognitive capacities for learning new things, being challenged to grow, and staying focused with our daily activities. Our emotional well-being includes our capacity for self-awareness and self-regulating of our emotions, being socially aware of others' emotions, and managing interpersonal relationships or challenging situations with resilience. Our spiritual well-being focuses on self-actualization and self-cultivation of our character and authentic nature in connection with a higher power, often referred to as Spirit, Nature, Universe, Source, or God of our knowing. Keys 3 through 6 will provide mindfulness practices for cultivating these capacities. These capacities are often skipped, but they are essential. They help us access our head, heart, and body intelligences, allowing us to engage more powerfully and authentically in our careers and relationships.

The outer circle of the map outlines the six areas of how we contribute to or what we do in the world. These areas include career; finances; primary relationship with significant other; relationships with family, friends, and colleagues; selfless service to underserved communities; and leisure time for travel, play, relaxation, and hobbies. The aim of this map is to help you align your physical, mental, emotional, and spiritual capacities with your experiences to fully embody and be congruent with your most authentic and powerful self. When you do your inner work, your life naturally falls into alignment with your well-being and life purpose. This is the secret sauce for unlocking your greatest potential.

Table 4.1: Life Compass Map

Life Compass Map Exercise

Now that you understand the Life Compass Map, begin rating your current level of satisfaction across the ten life areas on a scale of zero to ten, with zero being very dissatisfied and ten being very satisfied, and capture your answers in a notepad. There are no right or wrong answers. Be honest, listen to your intuition, and indicate where you fall on the scale across the ten life areas shown below. Next, assess where you want to be one year from now. Determine which areas you want to enhance or evolve to the next level. In the following chapters, you will learn best practices for growing in many of these areas, and create a roadmap for success that will lead you serendipitously to your vision.

1. Physical: physical health, energy levels, diet and lifestyle, cardio exercise, and mind-body practices (such as yoga and qigong)

2. Mental: mental health; cognitive capacities for learning and growth; mental agility for staying focused, clear, and relaxed at work

3. Emotional: emotional intelligence (self-awareness, self-management, social awareness, and relationship management) and emotional resilience during stressful and challenging situations

4. Spiritual: connection to a higher power or nature; self-study and self-actualization

5. Career: life work, vocation, growth, and creativity

6. Finances: money, savings, retirement, and purchases

7. Primary relationship: significant other or spouse

8. Other relationships: family, friends, boss, and colleagues

9. Leisure: travel, play, relaxation, and hobbies

10. Service: selfless service or contribution to underserved communities

Reflections

- What is your hero's journey? Map out the significant events, transitions, setbacks, insights, and choices in your career and life that have led you to where you are today.

- Identify your top five strengths. How can you amplify these strengths at work?

- Identify your top five weaknesses. How can you minimize your weaknesses and play more to your strengths at work?

- Define your top ten core values. What value do you want to experience more of in your career and life?

- What is your unique purpose? How might you lead with your purpose at work?

- Where do you envision your life and career five and ten years from now?

- What skills, education, and experience do you need to realize your vision?

- Life Compass Map: Across the ten life areas, where are you most satisfied in your life? Where are you least satisfied? Identify two areas you would like to change.

KEY #2

Put Your Oxygen Mask On First

Self-care is a generous act of kindness. It's about taking a stand for your personal needs instead of sacrificing them to please another.

In the midst of the 2020 global pandemic, practicing self-care was essential to stay healthy and resilient while global leaders and health-care professionals worked to develop a vaccine and mitigate the proliferation of patient cases or deaths. Self-care is not only essential in a pandemic, it's essential in navigating our career and life. In this chapter, I reveal the second key, *Put Your Oxygen Mask on First*, where we explore the myths and benefits of self-care, as well as practical self-care and time-management strategies to reset, recharge, and keep us rocking our purpose without burning out. It's essentially our life-rescue toolkit.

Jacqueline's Story

Jacqueline, a senior manager over a global business-operations team, supported leaders in delivering technology products to market. With over fifteen years in the company, she was recognized as a high performer, ready for the next level of promotion. She was known for managing complex customer engagements, developing strategic plans, and driving business results. Loyal, focused, collaborative, and a team player, Jacqueline worked long hours to meet business and stakeholder needs. Unfortunately, her unwavering focus to drive results gave her no time to build strategic partnerships with senior leaders to increase the visibility of her team's contributions to the business and position herself for a future promotion. Her taxing work left her exhausted, stressed, and unable to make the impact she wanted as a leader.

Jacqueline was ready to invest in her leadership growth and be promoted to the director-level within the next two years. During our coaching engagement, we recognized she was doing most of the critical work herself and not leveraging her team. She was overcommitting on projects, failing to maximize her team capacity due to trust issues, and not blocking time for strategic work or personal development. To ensure she stayed resilient and focused, using the tools outlined in this chapter, we crafted a self-care plan to increase her effectiveness and help her avoid burnout. Initially, she struggled with saying no to stakeholder requests and delegating to her team because they lacked core job skills. However, as she faced these insecurities and started taking action, she noticed some surprising results. She had more time and energy to get strategic work done, train her team to take on new projects, and negotiate more funding to deliver on customer requests. More importantly, she was happier, blocking time for self-care, and replenishing her energy.

Self-care encompasses everything from taking care of our basic needs for food, connection, and shelter to taking time to relax and feel emotionally, physically, and mentally balanced. It is the basis for our well-being. In some ways, self-care has gotten a bad rap in the workplace. It may be construed as selfish or not being a team player. In actuality, self-care is about the small moments and incremental habits we develop that allow us to reset and recharge to be more focused, pro-ductive, and present in relationships without feeling guilty about caring for our needs. It's not about choosing ourselves over others; rather, it's about taking care of ourselves so we can be more fully available without depleting our emotional reserves.

Most of us have traveled on an airplane and listened to the safety instructions. One of the directives is to put your oxygen mask on before attending to small children or other people. The reason this step is imperative is that if we tend to others first, we will most likely pass out from a lack of oxygen. Self-care is about putting our oxygen mask on first so we don't burn out. It's about tending to our personal needs first to reset our mental, emotional, and physical energy so we can have more of that energy to give generously to others.

Though self-care sounds simple, it's not always easy. It challenges our inherent beliefs regarding our self-worth and value. For instance, you may have learned in early childhood that saying no meant you were rude, selfish, or unkind, and you may have been disciplined by a parent, caretaker, or teacher. As an adult, this behavior of people-pleasing, of always saying yes, becomes ingrained in your brain chemistry. It drives how you build relationships, seek recognition, or become the go-to expert when others need assistance. This unhelpful belief may lead you to consistently exceed expectations, overcommit to work when you are exhausted, not have bandwidth or mental capacity, or take on larger responsibilities before you have mastered your current leadership role. You may not even be aware that you are overcommitted and stressed out until your family, friends, colleagues, or manager say something. Or, you get your annual physical exam results indicating you have high blood pressure, high cholesterol, or hypothyroidism. Fortunately, there is an easier way to achieve our career aspirations without sacrificing our personal needs or burning out. Experiment with these five strategies to enhance your energy, productivity, mental state, and effectiveness.

Prioritize Your Workload

Take time to assess your work priorities and other life activities. Use this 4D Model or a prioritization method of your preference. Writing down all your ideas and to-do lists on a notepad will declutter your mind and help you evaluate your activities more clearly. When our minds are full, it's difficult to prioritize, and we move into a scattered or busy mode versus truly being productive. When we are in control of our workload and aware of our priorities, we can more effectively manage incoming projects and requests.

- **Do** all activities that are urgent and important or delegate them to another team member.
- **Don't do** any activity that is unimportant or not urgent. Your time and energy will ultimately be wasted or undervalued.
- **Delegate** important activities to a direct report or another team member who is better equipped to manage that work. This helps your direct report grow, learn, make mistakes, and take on more responsibility with your oversight.
- **Defer** important nonurgent activities to give you and your team more time to deliver quality work.

Now that you understand how to prioritize your workload, let's discuss how to be more productive. A popular time-management principle is the 80/20 rule created by management expert Joseph Juran. He named this principle after the Italian economist Vilfredo Pareto, who observed that 80 percent of the income in Italy was received by 20 percent of the Italian population.[20] Essentially, this means that

80 percent of our results or outcomes come from 20 percent of our effort or input on specific activities. We often think we need to do everything assigned to us to demonstrate our competence and value. Unfortunately, this only leads to burnout and resentment over time. With the 4D model above, you can identify the activities that give you energy, provide the most impact, and are aligned with your goals, purpose, and vision. If you are spending a lot of time on activities that do not add value, such as unproductive meetings or irrelevant projects, it's time to deprioritize these activities from your work responsibilities. If you cannot stop current work projects, build a business case and share it with your manager, including the benefits these changes will bring and options for focusing on key strategic priorities to increase operational efficiency and profitability.

Research shows that the ideal time to focus on important work projects is in the morning. The brain is more clear, creative, and less distracted with the details of the day, such as meetings, emails, and personal needs. After a good night's sleep, we have more mental energy. Our metabolism is at peak performance in the morning. Most successful leaders do their most important work—strategic planning, important meetings, and creative projects—during this time. They use workouts, meditation, and other activities to prepare for the day and get their mental game in check. They leave the emails, less-important meetings, and informal conversations for later in the afternoon. They also take energy breaks every sixty to ninety minutes to recharge their bodies and minds.

Working from home may require more self-discipline to focus on your work priorities without getting distracted. Setting clear boundaries between work and life, such as creating a home office space or establishing work hours, will support you in maintaining physical and mental balance while delivering on projects. Productivity is not a one-size-fits-all.

Find a natural rhythm that inspires creativity and productivity without producing burnout.

Saying No

Saying no to others' requests can bring up a host of insecurities about our capabilities and relationships. You may be thinking, "If I say no, I will not be seen as a team player or a candidate for the next promotion." It's important to be courageous to say no to additional work or requests for the sake of your well-being. Especially, work that does not align to your team's priorities or you do not have the time or energy to execute well. Remember, this doesn't mean you are selfish or not a team player. It means you are a valuable and important person and your time and energy matter. If you live at the mercy of others' approval, you cannot be truly free or happy. Your self-worth does not depend on how much you do for others; it depends on you advocating for your well-being. Before you say yes, reflect on what you are saying no to. Perhaps saying yes to an extra work project means you won't be seeing your child's baseball game or attending a friend's wedding since you now have to work evenings and weekends to get the project done. While it can be wise to accept work projects that contribute to your long-term goals, be sure that other important areas of your life, especially health and relationships, aren't short-changed in the process.

Another reason it's difficult to say no is the fear of missing out, commonly known as FOMO. We are fortunate to have many possibilities to choose from in this digital world from international job assignments to exotic vacations. Our gut instinct is to say yes to these exciting experiences in fear we may miss out on a future opportunity: "If I don't go to the international conference in Italy, I will lose a chance of networking with key customers to help with my business." The problem we have with this strategy is we take on too much responsibility and become overloaded, causing more stress than reward. It's like going to an "all you can eat buffet" and piling your plate with a variety of delicious foods, only to find you can only digest a portion of the food. Instead, take time to choose a few top priorities you want to engage in for that month or year. You may need to deprioritize an important project to give space for another opportunity that will enrich your career. Or, you can schedule time to engage in those events or projects when you have more mental space and physical capacity. This will allow you to enjoy those activities without burning out or struggling to deliver on your commitments.

Here are four tips for saying no with empowerment and without feeling guilty:

- Be direct and clear: "No, I cannot take on this project right now."
- Be polite, kind, and thankful: "Thank you for asking and thinking of me for this project; however, my team and I do not have any bandwidth right now."
- Avoid apologizing or saying you will think about it when you do not want to do it.
- Avoid lying, since that leads to guilt, dishonesty, or avoidance of the person who asked for your time.

Block Focus Time

Managing multiple priorities and attending to conference calls all day can leave little time for self-reflection and strategic planning. It's difficult to be productive and creative when our minds are full of work deliverables, ideas or endless to-do lists. Blocking out "focus time" each week will allow you the time and mental space to get things done and work on more strategic projects. More time gives the space to build a plan for the next fiscal year, prepare a proposal on a new product offer, explore other job opportunities, or develop your leadership skills to get promoted. Here's the deal: When you schedule "focus time," do everything in your power not to let another stakeholder or team member force you to cancel that time slot. If your "focus time" conflicts with important team or customer meetings, find a time that is consistently available, such as Fridays, to keep your personal time sacred. Defining a powerful reason why this time is important will boost your motivation. You can also look for ways other team members can serve as a proxy for meetings rather than sacrificing your time.

Let Go of Stressors

When I struggled with chronic fatigue and burnout, my doctor encouraged me to examine the life stressors that were blocking me from regaining my health. When I got honest with myself, I had a lot of areas in my life, including habits and even relationships, that were unhealthy and creating tremendous stress. I had become an expert at tolerating situations instead of establishing healthy boundaries.

We all have stressors to contend with in life. These stressors can include long commutes, a manager who is not championing your success, coworkers who are undermining your efforts and don't have your back, eating unhealthy foods or skipping meals, or a significant other who is not honoring your needs and well-being. Make a list of everything that creates stress in your life and commit to taking action on a few or perhaps all of the items to reduce those stressors. This could mean you request to work from home multiple times a week; communicate openly and honestly your needs and experiences with your manager, coworkers, or significant other; eat healthy foods, drink less alcohol, reduce your use of stimulants, such as coffee and sugar; and exercise several times a week. This may be one of the most difficult self-care practices in the short-term; however, in the long-term, you will feel more energized, engaged, and empowered in your work and life.

Fill Your Joy Cup

The antidote to negative and stressful states is the cultivation of joy in your life. We often find ourselves consumed by our careers and personal lives and forget to do the things that bring us happiness. Over time, our busyness increases cortisol, a hormone made by the body's adrenal glands. Healthy cortisol levels reduce inflammation and regulate blood sugar and sleep. Cortisol is the body's main stress hormone in activating the fight-flight-or-freeze response. When we are constantly stressed, our cortisol becomes elevated, reducing the neurotransmitters serotonin and dopamine, which create a state of happiness. Consequently, our memory, focus, immune system, and other major bodily organs are negatively impacted.

A powerful way to overcome negative states is by finding ways to bring more joy into your life every day. This means doing activities that you love, make your heart smile, and make you feel alive. This can include hiking, connecting with nature, engaging in sports, spending time with family and friends, yoga, meditating, dancing, laughing, singing, painting, and playing a musical instrument. Once you come up with your list, take on a thirty-day challenge to do one activity that brings you joy every day. Over time, you will create new habits and neural pathways that will stimulate more joy, aliveness, health, and well-being.

In the following chapters, we'll talk about additional self-care strategies such as mind-body practices like yoga, qigong, and meditation, cardio exercise, nutritional lifestyle changes, and how to consistently get a good night's sleep.

Reflections

- What ways are you sacrificing your personal needs at work and in your personal life?
- What boundaries can you establish to nurture your self-care needs (putting your oxygen mask on first) and serve others more generously?
- What projects or requests can you "say no" to have more mental balance and deliver on your promises?
- How might you prioritize your workload to align with your priorities and capacity?
- Where can you block more "focus time" to get important tasks done?
- What stressors do you need to let go of to have more energy and fulfillment?
- What activities bring you joy?

KEY #3

Recharge and Nourish Your Body

Slowing down is not an act of laziness. It's an act of self-compassion that recharges your energy to meet life demands with grounded balance, resilience, and presence.

Jacob was a senior manager leading the artificial-intelligence-regulatory policies at a social media company. He was intelligent, energetic, optimistic, compassionate, and laser-focused on building a high-performing team that maximized their strengths while delivering exceptional results. He was a wizard at solving complex problems, building strong partnerships, and creating collaborative and trusting team environments.

To maintain his stellar performance, Jacob worked long hours and spent over half that time traveling to meet with key partners, leaders, and government officials. He often took our coaching calls while driving to the airport or walking to his next meeting. Although Jacob was masterful at his job and was on the fast track to becoming a director, he was overwhelmed, tired, and not fully leveraging his team's capabilities to scale and elevate his leadership influence.

During a coaching call, Jacob shared how excited he was for his upcoming "recharge" retreat. Upon working for the company for five years, employees received a five-week sabbatical to reset and unplug completely from work. Jacob did exactly that. He arranged a direct report to cover his responsibilities. He rested, visited family, traveled, exercised, and engaged in activities he loved. The positive results of his sabbatical were evident when Jacob returned to work. He was more present, focused, confident, and felt unstoppable. He was ready to lead a larger team with broader scope and to coach that team to be more self-sufficient in delivering the day-to-day activities. He came back *recharged*.

In this chapter, we delve into the fourth key, *Recharge and Nourish Your Body*. We explore the causes and the science behind stress and how to manage stress more effectively, as well as the best practices to recharge, strengthen, and nourish our body and well-being. These mind-body strategies help us optimize our performance at work while preventing burning out.

Stress in the workplace is inevitable. Understanding how stress works and where it comes from allows us to manage it more effectively. Stress is our body's natural reaction to external or internal stressors. When the brain detects a stressor that appears life-threatening, it initiates a series of biological responses. It pushes blood to our large muscle groups, releases stress hormones, and raises our heart rate, blood pressure, and blood sugar, forcing us to fight, flee—or freeze if the situation is too overwhelming.

Why does the brain initiate these biological responses? UCLA clinical professor and psychiatrist Daniel Siegel's book, *Mindful Brain*, describes the brain's neurobiological processes and how the three major regions of the brain—brainstem, limbic region, and neocortex—work synergistically during a stressful life event.[21] The brain stem or reptilian brain, the oldest and most primitive region of our brain, regulates physiological functions such as breathing, heart rate, body temperature, and balance. Some researchers suggest the brainstem, in conjunction with the limbic region, stimulates our reaction to threat, causing a fight-flight-or-freeze stress response. It is designed to create states of safety when we are threatened with situations that overwhelm our nervous system, such as a chronic health condition, death of a family member, tragic car accident, or mountain lion attack. Our brain is designed to be on guard against any danger or threat and to keep us safe. When the situation is too overwhelming, the brain will initiate a freeze response, where we become completely immobile. This is imperative for life-threatening situations, but when we're managing our modern daily activities or working collaboratively with others, it becomes limiting and self-defeating. A negativity bias about our experiences is created and stored in our brain's limbic region for future reference.

The limbic region, often known as the "emotional brain," regulates our emotional response, our memory, and our hormonal response via the amygdala, hippocampus, and hypothalamus, respectively. The amygdala assigns meaning to the stressor based on a past traumatic experience, which activates a reactive, emotional response. Research shows memory lives in our nervous system. When we feel threatened, helpless, overwhelmed, or extremely angry, our autonomic nervous system engages. The autonomic nervous system regulates bodily functions such as breathing, heart rate, digestion, blood pressure, sweating, and sexual arousal. It has two main components integral in stress regulation: 1) the sympathetic nervous system, connected to our internal organs to the brain, regulates our fight-or-flight response during stressful situations; and 2) parasympathetic nervous system, connected to cranial, vagus and lumbar spinal nerves, regulates our rest and digest as well as the freeze response. You can think of the sympathetic nervous system as pressing down on the "gas pedal" of a motor vehicle and the parasympathetic nervous system as putting on the "brake".[22] Multiple biological functions get activated during stress. When the sympathetic nervous system kicks off the fight-or-flight response, the hypothalamic-pituitary-adrenal axis of the limbic region begins firing. This triggers the hypothalamus to send hormonal messages to the pituitary gland to stimulate the adrenal glands, releasing the hormones cortisol and adrenaline to help the body mobilize and escape perceived danger. Our hearts begin to race, palms get sweating, pupils dilate, and blood gets pushed to the large muscles and organs to prepare us to fight or flee from the person or situation. This is why people often exhibit superhuman strength in life-and-death emergencies, such as lifting a car to save a child's life.

The advanced region of our brain, the neocortex, regulates our major body systems and supports are rational thinking, planning, decision-making, and executive functions. It's in the prefrontal cortex, located behind the forehead, where we form ideas, concepts, and insights, including moral judgment and sense of self. The problem is, when blood is released to the lower extremities, the prefrontal cortex doesn't receive a sufficient amount of oxygen or blood for us to think rationally or critically in the moment. Psychologist Daniel Goleman calls this an "amygdala hijack."[23] When stress triggers strong fear, anger, or aggression, the amygdala overrides the functioning of the frontal lobes and activates the fight-flight-or-freeze response, which is usually highly emotional and exaggerated when compared to the actual situation.

Psychotherapist and trauma expert Peter Levine asserts that when our biological system is overwhelmed and we are not able to process and release a stressful event, the brain stores it as a memory to protect us from future danger.[24] During these events, the brain initiates a freeze response, to keep you completely still or even shutdown, to protect you from danger. You see this in animals pretending to be dead to survive a predator attack.[25] Hence, the unprocessed stress becomes a traumatic memory stored in the body until a present-day trigger causes that memory to resurface. For example, after tumbling down a thirty-foot ravine in my car accident, it was difficult for me to drive up a narrow mountain road without experiencing anxiety and my arms freezing at the wheel. It took years to overcome this post-traumatic stress response, but over time and with deliberate practice driving up mountain roads, I finally discharged it from my body. Fortunately, the brain is brilliant. When we feel overly stressed, the parasympathetic nervous system kicks in, signaling us to rest and slow down. This can show up as crashing for an afternoon nap or sleeping a full day to rebalance after returning from an international trip. Another way to unhook the stress response is dia-phragmatic breathing and walking in nature, which I describe in detail below. These exercises help reduce our heart rate and regulate our ner-vous system to a calmer state as quickly as ten minutes.

When stress happens only occasionally, the body can easily regulate to a state of homeostasis or equilibrium, with no long-lasting health effects. However, when stress becomes chronic, lingering for months and even years, persistent surges of the stress response and elevated epi-nephrine and cortisol levels become maladaptive, making it difficult to rebalance to a calm state without stress-reduction practices and tools. Long-term stress can lead to physical problems such as digestive issues, inflammation, hormone imbalances, diabetes, and heart disease, or mental problems, such as anxiety and depression.

The good news is that we can overcome stress and retrain the body to be more resilient. When we understand our biological response and the signs of stress, we can build more self-awareness and self-compassion the next time we experience a threat to our well-being, such as being laid off from a job, a global health or financial crisis, difficulties in relationships, or even tough conversations. We can manage stress through consistent mind-fulness strategies, such as restful sleep; mind-body practices, such as yoga and qigong; cardio exercise; exposure to nature and sunshine; and organic, whole-food nutrition. When we engage in diaphragmatic breathing through yoga, qigong, and meditation, we rebalance our nervous system. Diaphragmatic breathing stimulates the vagus nerve, the autonomic nervous system's longest nerve, which runs from the neck to the abdomen. This nerve is largely responsible for turning off the fight-flight-or-freeze response and activating the calm-and-relax response to regulate many biological functions, such as heart rate, digestion, and blood pressure.

How does the brain and body communicate? Science shows that we have a gut-brain connection that is a key factor in our physical, emotional, and mental well-being. This is the enteric nervous system or second brain which bidirectionally communicates with the brain and neuroendocrine system. Comprised of 100 million neurons, it works independently from the central nervous system and plays an integral role in our digestion, mood, health, and the way we think. This gut-brain connection also manages the key neurotransmitters that contribute to our feelings of happiness: serotonin and dopamine.[26]

Have you ever had "butterflies in your stomach" or experienced a "gut feeling"? These expressions are examples how our gastrointestinal tract communicates through emotion. Feelings such as anger, anxiety, excitement, and sadness, can trigger symptoms in the gut. When we experience stress, you may experience symptoms such as bloating and constipation, along with overwhelm and anxiety. To combat the stress, the stress hormone cortisol gets released along with the parasympathetic nervous system to regulate metabolism, blood pressure, and blood sugar.

By listening to our gut instincts or physiological symptoms, we can better manage our energy levels, prevent chronic ailments, and curb the signs of burnout quickly. Like a computer, our brain and nervous system have the ability to uninstall and reinstall a new operating system that reinforces new positive habits and ways for regulating stress that restore our well-being. Next time you are working long hours trying to meet a deadline, take a pause and listen to your gut intelligence. It may be signaling signs for a break, exercise, or unplugging from technology and work altogether. In this next section, you will discover best practices for staying physically, emotionally, and mentally balanced and achieving peak performance in your career.

Restful Sleep

"It is estimated that 50 to 70 million Americans experience sleep-related problems." The Center for Disease Control says, "Insufficient sleep is a public health epidemic."[27] Sleep represents one-third of every person's life and has a tremendous impact on how we function at work and in our lives. It is as vital as the air we breathe and the food we eat and affects various aspects of mental and physical health, including productivity, emotional balance, a strong immune system, creativity, and mental clarity. Demanding schedules, frequent traveling, or life transitions can disrupt sleep and take a substantial toll on our mood, energy, and mental acuity, reducing our ability to handle stress and wreaking havoc on our health. Sleep enables the brain to oversee the biological maintenance that allows us to work, learn, innovate, and communicate at peak performance levels throughout the day.

What factors determine a restful sleep? First, the brain has structures and chemicals that produce states of sleeping and wakefulness called circadian rhythms—our body's internal clock. These rhythms are established during the first months of life and control daily biological patterns, including body temperature, blood pressure, and the release of hormones. Sleep is dictated by circadian rhythms that are the strongest between midnight and dawn and between the afternoon hours of 1:00 p.m. and 3:00 p.m. These sleep cycles can determine your quality of sleep, which is essential to your well-being.

During a sleep cycle, the body goes through many stages to rest, repair, and rejuvenate itself for the next day. Sleep research shows that to maintain optimal health, an adult needs seven to nine hours of sleep, while children and teens need more for healthy development. Scientists suggest that one to two hours at the deep-sleep stage is optimal for the body to repair tissue and bones, strengthen the immune system, and replenish energy levels. On the other hand, the REM, or rapid eye movement, stage, which occurs ninety minutes after falling asleep, is essential for the brain to process and retain memories and knowledge and elevate our mood and mental states for the day. It's during the REM phase that our brain develops the important neural connections key to our mental and overall well-being and health. When these sleep states are compromised, we do not get the quality of sleep we need to feel happy, productive, present, and fully engaged in our lives and relationships.

Another key ingredient of restful sleep is sufficient levels of melatonin, a hormone released by the brain's pineal gland. This hormone works in harmony with the body's circadian rhythms. Melatonin kicks in when it's dark and peaks around 10:00 p.m., signaling the body it's time to sleep. Electronic devices, such as smartphones, laptops, or tablets, emit a blue light that decreases melatonin and impacts our quality of sleep. Getting enough quality sleep may be challenging for high performers who cannot disconnect from work or constantly check their messages. Here are some key signs that you are sleep deprived:

- You need an alarm clock to wake up on time, or you feel sluggish getting out of bed, or you are tired in the afternoon.
- You feel drowsy or fall asleep easily in meetings and warm rooms, after heavy meals, or while driving.
- You nap during the day, sleep on the weekends, or fall asleep within five minutes of going to bed.

Sleep deprivation can show up physically and mentally as fatigue, lethargy, lack of motivation, moodiness, depression, difficulty concentrating, and memory problems. And it contributes to more severe health problems, such as stroke, diabetes, heart disease, or Alzheimer's.[28]

The key to getting a good night's sleep is to create good sleep hygiene. Here are ten best practices from leading sleep experts:[29]

1. Commit to a regular sleep schedule—go to bed and get up at the same time every day. Adults should get to sleep between 10:00 p.m. and 11:00 p.m. to take advantage of the melatonin boost.

2. Get regular exercise—thirty minutes or more on most days, but not too close to bedtime. Strenuous workouts in the evening increase body temperature, making it harder to fall asleep.

3. Avoid stimulants such as caffeine, alcohol, and sugar four hours before bedtime.

4. Avoid eating fatty meals or drinking lots of fluids two to three hours before bedtime.

5. Avoid any electronic devices and bright screens two to three hours before bed. The blue light shifts sleep rhythms, reducing melatonin levels, making it difficult to sleep.

6. Reduce stressors as noted in the previous chapter.

7. Improve your sleep environment, creating a dark, quiet, cool bedroom, with a comfortable mattress and bedding.

8. Wind down with an evening ritual, such as a warm bath, meditation, reading with a dim light, listening to music, slow breathing while lying down, or restorative yoga.

9. Write down any feelings of worry and anxiety in a note-book to address the next day, when they will be much easier to resolve.

10. Check with your doctor for any medical reasons for poor sleep, such as apnea, diabetes, heart disease, or any other physical problems.

Mind-Body Practices

Practicing yoga was a saving grace when I was in graduate school while maintaining a full-time job, and it's kept me balanced and resilient while working in fast-paced environments as a global business leader. Originally taught in India over five thousand years ago, modern yoga has become popular not only with workout enthusiasts but with business executives, athletes, and celebrities hoping to gain vast health benefits from the practice. Yoga goes beyond building a strong, flexible body. It's about cultivating a deeper mind-body awareness. When we heal, relax, and balance the physical body, we bring more focus and stillness to the mind. In the ancient Indian language of Sanskrit, yoga means "to yoke" or "union." It helps us integrate the mind and body to our true nature. Most yoga classes are rooted in the hatha yoga tradition, which focuses on a series of asanas (postures) and mindful breathing to prepare the body for meditation.

Given the many styles of mind-body practices, it can be tricky to determine which one is best for your body. For our purposes, we will focus on three categories of mind-body practices to help you choose which practice will best serve your body and well-being: 1) flow-based yoga, such as vinyasa and ashtanga, which link breath to movement through a series of postures to build strength, flexibility, balance, and alignment; 2) therapeutic yoga, such as restorative, yin and yoga nidra, which are designed to alleviate physical and mental stress through deep relaxation and muscle and connective-tissue release; and 3) qi-gong, which restores, balances and elevates our physical, emotional, and mental energies.

Flow-Based Yoga

For those who enjoy a rigorous workout that builds strength and flexibility, and breaks a sweat, Vinyasa or Ashtanga are your ideal practices. Vinyasa is an intelligent, creative, and seamless flow of postures where you synchronize your breath with each posture and move toward to an inner harmony with your body and mind. Using sun salutations, standing, seated, hip-opening, and inversion poses, this yoga helps build strength, balance, steadiness, flexibility, and resilience to meet the demands and joys of life.

Ashtanga yoga, which means "eight limbs," focuses on purifying body and mind and cultivating more mind-body awareness. Through a dynamic, vinyasa-based sequence, it connects the breath through a structured series of forty-one sequential poses, including standing, seated, and inverted. This style of yoga is either guided by a teacher or self-led. The aim is to build a progressive, safe, and sustainable practice that facilitates continuous awakening from old patterns and habits.

Therapeutic-Based Yoga

A perfect complement to the flow-based yoga practices are the therapeutic yoga styles. These are useful to release the stressors from the day, replenish our energy, and prepare the body for a restful night's sleep.

Restorative yoga is a relaxing style of yoga aimed to rebalance the nervous system and deepen our self-awareness. It's a practice of slowing down and releasing body tension from the stresses of life. Using props, such as bolsters, blankets, straps, and blocks, this practice guides students to hold poses for five to ten minutes while giving the benefits of deep, passive stretching. Through a slow sequence of postures and conscious breathing, it activates the parasympathetic nervous system, which allows the body to deeply relax and regulate to a calm state. With sustained practice, this form of yoga can enhance your mood, mental clarity, quality of sleep, and immune system while cultivating more self-compassion.

Yin yoga is a slow, soothing, and meditative style of yoga. It targets the deep connective tissues, bones, joints, fascia, and ligaments in the body. This practice also uses props and holds poses up to four minutes to stimulate the different acupressure points in traditional Chinese medicine. The benefits of this practice include reduced stress, increased circulation, relief of tension, improved flexibility, and a deeper body-mind awareness of our physical, mental, and emotional states. It also activates the parasympathetic nervous system through diaphragmatic breathing, which supports the regulation of our blood pressure, sleep, digestion, hormones, and immune function.

Yoga nidra, meaning "yogic sleep", is a practice that induces total physical, mental, and emotional relaxation. While lying flat on your back, the teacher gently guides you to scan and sense each body part from your toes to your head while maintaining conscious awareness. With every breath you are letting go of tension and surrendering to a deeper state of relaxation. This guided meditation activates four main stages of brain wave activity—beta, alpha, theta, and delta to achieve a "hypnagogic state"—a state between wakefulness and sleep. The deep relaxation helps balance the sympathetic and parasympathetic nervous systems as well as the left and right brain hemispheres. Research studies show yoga nidra helps stabilize blood sugar levels, alleviate pre-menstrual syndrome symptoms, depression, and anxiety and combat post-traumatic stress disorder (PTSD). Thirty minutes of this practice is similar to two hours of restful sleep.[30]

Qigong

Qigong is an ancient Chinese practice that dates back five thousand years. It improves one's mental and physical health by integrating posture, movement, breathing technique, self-massage, sound, and focused intent. Qigong uses gentle, slow movements that are repeated to strengthen, stretch, and warm the tendons, ligaments, and muscles; tonify vital organs and connective tissues; promote circulation of body fluids (blood, synovial, lymph); and improve awareness of how the body moves through space. Research studies have shown qigong to be effective in helping heal life challenges ranging from high blood pressure and chronic illness to emotional frustration, mental stress, and spiritual crisis.

Below are two simple breathing practices you can use to regulate your nervous system and cultivate more mental balance, relaxation, and focus anytime of the day.

Mind-Body Reset

This breathing practice is designed to reset your mental and physical balance and quickly help you shift to a calm, relaxed, and grounded state. This is a great alternative for busy people who do not have time for yoga and meditation practices.

- Sit in a comfortable, relaxed position on a cushion or chair with your spine tall and your neck, shoulders, arms, and body relaxed; your feet firmly on the ground or crossed legged if sitting on the ground or cushion; your hands resting in your lap; your eyes gently closed.
- Bring your attention to your breath. Meet your breath where it's at without controlling or engaging it in any way. Observe your breath as a neutral observer. Breathe

in and out through your nostrils with your attention on
your lower abdomen.

- Inhale slowly counting to five and holding your breath
for a count of five.

- Exhale slowly counting to five and pausing for a count of
five.

- Do this diaphragmatic breathing for ten cycles until you
feel calm, relaxed, and at ease.

Alternate Nostril Breathing

This breathing practice, known as *nadi shodhana pranayama*, is pri-
marily aimed at clearing and purifying the subtle channels of the mind
and body while balancing the brain hemispheres to create more mental
balance and stillness. Research shows that yogic breathing exercises, or
pranayamas, can enhance neurocognitive, psychophysiological, respira-
tory, and metabolic functions.[31] It's best done on an empty stomach and
not when sick or congested.

To practice alternate nostril breathing:

- Sit in a comfortable, relaxed position on a cushion or
chair with your spine tall and your neck, shoulders,
arms, and body relaxed to the best of your ability.

- Place your left hand on your left knee and lift your right
hand toward your nose.

- Exhale completely and then close your right nostril with
your right thumb.

- Inhale through your left nostril and then close the left
nostril with your index finger.

- Release your thumb on the right nostril and exhale
through the right nostril.

- Inhale through the right nostril and then close the right nostril with your thumb.
- Exhale through the left nostril and repeat the cycle.
- Continue this breathing practice for five minutes.

I often personalize yoga, meditation, and breathing practices to support my client's specific needs. For example, Julie was a top health-care executive who wanted to build more body awareness and reduce the stress and anxiety that came with the demands of her role. With a high IQ, she was astute at problem-solving, researching industry trends, having tough conversations, and getting things done. She even engaged in vinyasa yoga classes to burn off her stress during the week. During our engagement, I suggested yin yoga, body-awareness meditation, and breathing practices to help regulate her nervous system and culti-vate more inner calm and balance. This allowed her to sense and track her body sensations when she was stressed or not in agreement with an important business decision. With consistent practice and through journaling her insights, Julie noticed a big difference in her energy and productivity levels and how she was more present, patient, and available for her team, colleagues, and family.

Cardio Exercise

Cardio exercises, such as walking, swimming, gardening, running, cycling, and playing soccer, are an excellent way to elevate heart rate, circulate blood, and strengthen muscles. Health professionals recom-mend getting 150 minutes of moderate cardio exercise or seventy-five minutes of vigorous activity each week. Research shows that aerobic exercise also improves cardiovascular health (e.g., lowers blood pressure, healthy cholesterol levels); enhances mental health and self-esteem; regulates blood-sugar and insulin levels; reduces chronic back pain, specifically with low-impact activities like swimming and aqua aerobics; and improves sleep quality.[32] When we exercise, our body releases chemicals called endorphins that interact with brain receptors to promote positive feelings and reduce pain in the body. These endorphins create the feeling, known as a "runner's high." I've seen leaders run or exercise during lunchtime and return to the office renewed, energized, and ready to conquer the remaining demands of the day.

Nature

Being outdoors is nature's medicine for relieving stress and experiencing more joy and inner peace. Our affinity toward nature is genetic and deeply rooted in our human evolution. In his book *Last Child in the Woods*, Richard Louv shares how we are experiencing a "nature deficit disorder," or a loss of connection to our natural environment.[33] Staying close to nature improves our physical, mental, and spiritual well-being and makes us feel alive, grounded, and restored. Often, urbanization, technology, and social media reduce or eliminate our exposure to nature. Studies show that being out in nature, whether walking, hiking, cycling, or running, improves mood, mental clarity, immunity with increased vitamin D levels (increasing white-blood-cell levels), and keeps our brain cells nourished and healthy.[34] Although sunshine has gotten a bad rap due to overexposure and skin cancer, it is the best natural source of vitamin D. One study found that thirty minutes of midday summer sun exposure in Oslo, Norway, was equivalent to consuming ten thousand to twenty thousand IU of vitamin D. To maintain healthy blood levels, aim for ten to thirty minutes of midday sunlight several times a week. Your exposure time will depend on your skin sensitivity and skin color; check with your doctor. Low vitamin-D levels are linked to health concerns such as osteoporosis, cancer, depression, and muscle weakness.[35]

Forest bathing—walking in the woods and soaking in the fresh oxygen—regulates the nervous system, heart rate, cortisol levels, circadian rhythms, and digestion.[36] In one study, researchers looked at the brain activity of healthy people after they walked in an urban setting for ninety minutes. They found that those who walked through the city had lower levels of activity in the prefrontal cortex and repetitive thoughts and negative emotions. When people are depressed or under high levels of stress, the prefrontal cortex malfunctions, creating continuous looping of negative thinking. They also found that when people engaged with natural spaces, basking in the beauty, sounds, and oxygen of the forest or coastal beaches, they receive therapeutic benefits, such as lower blood pressure and cortisol levels, which calm the body's stress response. Find time to go outdoors. Run on a dirt trail, walk in a park with grass and trees, hike in the woods, walk barefoot on dirt (commonly called "earthing"), or garden or do yard work to boost your health and well-being.

Nutrition

Given our fast-paced lifestyle, we sometimes barely have time to eat, particularly a healthy, nutritional, balanced meal. Research shows that poor nutrition and underlying health conditions contribute greatly to the vicious cycle of stress and burnout.

In my twenties, my go-to diet consisted of high-carb fast-foods, soda, and beer. Sadly, I learned in my thirties that eating this way was killing my digestion and overall health. After running a gamut of blood tests, my doctor shared that if I continued my current diet and lifestyle, I would likely have cancer by forty. Talk about a wake-up call. Thereafter, I was more motivated to change my diet and make necessary lifestyle changes to maintain my health and longevity. Over the last twenty years, I've tried a variety of diets, including vegetarian, vegan, whole-food, Mediterranean, blood-type, ketogenic, Ayurveda, and Paleo. I found that what worked for my constitution was an organic, grass-fed, anti-inflammatory, whole-food diet with generous portions of seasonal vegetables, low-glycemic fruits, and beans, and small portions of grass-fed meat, poultry, eggs, and no grains, sugar, or dairy. Although my diet seems restrictive, it's liberated me from debilitating chronic fatigue, digestive issues, and long-term disease.

Functional-medicine doctor and leading nutrition expert Dr. Mark Hyman offers evidence-based recommendations for eating a healthy, anti-inflammatory diet while maintaining peak performance, combining the best of the Paleo and vegan diets.[37] Having suffered his own chronic health condition, Dr. Hyman has dedicated his entire career to researching and creating food-based solutions to heal chronic-health, stress-related, and autoimmune disorders and is now one of the leading experts in the functional medicine and food revolution. Some of his key research found that our food and farming practices have been compromised with pesticides, additives, chemicals, antibiotics, and genetically modified protocols that increase production and minimize cost. Consequently, soils are depleted of rich minerals and filled with toxic chemicals and pesticides, such as glyphosate, which is found in Roundup. The food our parents and ancestors ate, such as corn, wheat, soy, meat, and chicken, are now adulterated, significantly reducing nutrient value and causing health risks. Thank goodness for local farmers who are dedicated to regenerating their soils, producing organic foods, and avoiding these conventional, unhealthy food practices. Yes, this is a topic large in scope. My aim is to equip you with the latest research to help you stay informed, healthy, and strong throughout your adult life and avoid a future diagnosis of a life-threatening disease. Knowing this information in my late twenties would have saved me tens of thousands of dollars along with years of suffering.

In Dr. Mark Hyman's book, *Food: What the Heck Should I Eat?*, you will find key guidelines on what foods are best to eat and what foods to avoid to strengthen your immune system and protect your body from disease. I suggest working with a functional medicine or medical doctor trained in nutrition and getting tested to personalize your health plan. Each body constitution and health condition requires different foods to maintain optimal physical and mental health. Below are nine key nutrition and mindful guidelines I use to maintain optimal health and well-being.

- Buy organic, local, grass-fed, wild, sustainably harvested, pasture-raised, non-genetically modified (GMO) foods that are USDA certified if possible.

- Avoid conventional foods harvested with pesticides, antibiotics, and hormones and which are genetically modified (GMO). Avoid any chemicals, additives, preservatives, dyes, artificial sweeteners, or junk ingredients or ingredients that are difficult to pronounce, such as butylated hydroxytoluene.

- Based on the USDA 2020 report, you should avoid the conventional dirty-dozen foods due to high pesticide residues. Where possible, always buy these organic: strawberries, spinach, kale, nectarines, apples, grapes, peaches, cherries, pears, tomatoes, celery, and potatoes. The following foods have the lowest amount of pesticide residue if you cannot find the organic varieties: avocados, pineapple, onions, papaya, sweet peas, eggplant, asparagus, cauliflower, cantaloupes, broccoli, mushrooms, cabbage, honeydew melon, and kiwi.[38]

- Prepare your own foods several times a week or find an organic food service. Dr. Hyman's book, *Food: What the*

Heck Should I Eat?, provides comprehensive information on food industry practices, food preparation, and the latest research on what specific foods to eat and avoid to stay healthy.

- Drink plenty of purified water to keep your mind and body working optimally. Our bodies are approximately 60 percent water. Some health authorities commonly recommend drinking eight, eight-ounce glasses of water a day. While others suggest sipping water throughout the day. It's best to check with your doctor about the right amount of water for your body type to stay hydrated.

- Get tested to identify any harmful bacteria, viruses, pathogens, heavy metals, and gut, liver, or hormonal imbalances. These tests will reveal what foods and protocols can help with your specific health situation.

- Practice intermittent fasting, where you fast during a sixteen-hour window and compress eating time within the remaining eight hours. It's called the "sixteen-eight method." You can vary this to be a thirteen- to sixteen-hour window for fasting and eight to eleven hours for eating to get the health benefits and follow your natural rhythm. If you want the benefits of autophagy, many experts suggest fasting beyond eighteen hours. Autophagy is the body's way of cleaning out damaged cells to regenerate newer, healthier cells. Whichever fasting method you try, avoid reducing calories during your eating window unless your goal is to lose weight. Intermittent fasting allows the body to repair at a deeper level, often improving fat digestion and cellular aging as well as reducing blood-sugar and insulin levels. There are many variations of this ancient healing practice. Diet variation combined with fasting builds metabolic flexibility and resiliency during times of stress and illness. These fasting methods are easy to implement, less calorie restrictive, and allow for flexibility in planning meals with family, friends, or at business events and meetings. Check out Dr. Jason Fung's books for more details about fasting and the impressive health benefits.[39]

- Take time to enjoy your meals. To create healthier eating habits, try these mindful tips: eat your foods in a relaxing place without distractions, chew your food slowly (roughly thirty times), notice the textures and flavors, give gratitude for your food, unplug from electronic devices, and be fully present whether alone or in the company of other people. We often eat under stress, so pausing and checking in to see how we are feeling provides valuable information about our mental and emotional states.

- Create healthy snacks you can eat at work, when traveling, at social events, or anytime you don't have access to healthy foods.

Taking the time to recharge, strengthen, and nourish your body and well-being will optimize your performance at work, prevent burnout, and help you master your busy mind. If you were dissatisfied with the state of your physical, emotional, and mental well-being from the Life Compass Map exercise, these strategies will accelerate your results. Getting quality sleep is essential in rebuilding your energy and stamina, reducing stress, and regulating your nervous system. Since these tools work harmoniously, augment your health goals with yoga and qigong practices, cardio exercise (especially in nature), and a healthy diet. This will enhance your performance, resilience, happiness at work, and overall health and longevity. A recharged, nourished, and healthy body helps create a relaxed, focused, and creative mind. Now, let's explore the reasons behind the monkey mind and how to enhance your mental performance.

Reflections

- How are you recharging and nourishing your body today?
- What rituals or practices would best support you getting a good night's sleep?
- What mind-body practices, cardio exercises, and nutritional habits would best support your health and well-being?

KEY #4
Master the Monkey Mind

When we calm the restless mind, we experience deep
silence, stillness, and spaciousness—opening
the doorway to our infinite potential.

Virginia was an emerging leader for a customer experience team
with a multinational technology company. She was a strategic, passionate, hardworking, loyal leader. Always saying "yes" to more responsibility to support business priorities and advance her career. She was
known for building high-performing teams, collaborative partnerships,
and new processes to improve operational efficiencies. When her team
underwent major organizational changes, she was worried and unclear
on how to maintain the same team performance levels and morale while
keeping up with her work and life demands. Virginia felt extremely
overwhelmed, out of balance, and spent hours thinking about how to
change this situation. To top it off, she had a young child with health
issues that required her constant energy and attention.

During our coaching engagement, she wanted to learn how to calm
her busy, overthinking mind and find the work-life balance she once
enjoyed in her career. We focused on reframing her negative mindsets and
cultivating a more relaxed, focused, and positive outlook to better reprior-
itize her work and leverage her team's capabilities. She initially struggled

with maintaining a daily practice, but she persisted. If she missed a day, she began again. After three months of consistent mindfulness training, she felt more confident and balanced as a leader. She built more team trust by listening more, reprioritized her workload, said no to new requests when she was overcommitted, and established boundaries between work and life priorities. When she felt overwhelmed, she did her mindfulness practice rather than be distracted by her overthinking mind. She now enjoys quality time for self-reflection, strategic planning, family, meditating, and exercise. By taking personal accountability for her circumstances, she enhanced her performance and well-being—experiencing more inner peace and joy.

Master the Monkey Mind is the fifth key. The "monkey mind" is a Buddhist term that means to be unsettled, restless, or confused. It is a metaphor for our minds jumping from thought to thought with non-stop chatter, similar to wild monkeys swinging from tree to tree. Our minds tend to attach to the endless to-do items, painful memories, negative judgments, and worst-case scenarios. This constant internal chatter activates the reptilian and limbic regions of the brain, bringing up memories that cause us to doubt our abilities and stop us from achieving our goals. In this chapter, we will further investigate the science, research, and reasons behind the monkey mind, negative thought patterns, and why we cling to negative experiences. We will explore evidence-based strategies for creating more self-awareness, and shifting negative mindsets to positive mindsets to unlock our innate intelligence and alleviate suffering.

Inside the Monkey Mind

What causes this internal chatter? Some people refer to the monkey mind as the ego mind. To understand the ego, we need to understand the human psyche. According to neurologist Sigmund Freud's personality theory, the human psyche is structured into three states of awareness: id, superego, and ego. The id is the instinctual, nonrational, primitive, and unconscious part of our psyche that seeks pleasure to satisfy basic urges, needs and desires, such as sex and food. It is present at birth and linked to the brain's reptilian and limbic regions. Often referred as our instinctual drives, this level of awareness seeks instant gratification and is the driving force for getting our needs met in the world. When our needs are not met, we can become tense, anxious, or angry and create a story around this experience: "I never get what I want" or "Life is unfair." The superego, on the other hand, is our moral conscience from an internalized parental authority. Often referred to as the "inner critic"—the judging and critical part of the psyche. It sets high or unrealistic expectations of how we should think, feel, and behave. It creates an imaginary ideal self to ensure we do what is right, acceptable, and perfect according to societal norms. Its role is to control our instinctual biological impulses for pleasure and instant gratification. When we fall short of our ideal self, we may punish ourselves through guilt or self-critical talk: "I am stupid," "I am not enough" or "I should have known better." This self-talk can block us from achieving our goals and cause unnecessary suffering.

Fortunately, the ego is the rational and realistic part of our conscious mind, residing in the pre-frontal cortex. It arbitrates between the id and superego, and tests internal assumptions based on the reality of the external world. We formulate a self-image or sense of self in the first three years of life, based on observations of our parents' behaviors and external environment. The internal conflict between the id, ego, and superego in our psyche causes the monkey-mind chatter. We create a distorted or false sense of self to keep ourselves safe and in control of our situations to avoid perceived danger. The ego is essential to our human existence and functioning as a healthy adult. It often gets a bad reputation as being a "trickster," "taskmaster" or the core reason for our suffering. This is partially true when we refer to the underdeveloped, overinflated, or wounded aspects of our psyche (id or superego). But, it's not the whole picture. It's our identification and attachment to these separate parts that create suffering. We may overinflate our self-image by thinking we are the smartest person in our field, creating a sense of superiority and arrogance. Or, we may undervalue our self-image by thinking we are stupid and have nothing to offer, creating a sense of inferiority or insecurity.

From a developmental psychology perspective, to grow to the next level and individuate as healthy human beings and adults we need to understand, heal, and integrate these fragmented parts of our psyche. When these parts are integrated, we can more clearly hear the voice of pure awareness. Awareness is the pure consciousness or innate intelligence that resides in the center of our being or neuro-physiological system. Its nature is unchanging and undifferentiated, meaning it is not an isolated self. This awareness is often known as the soul, presence, essence, or true self. The secret to mastering the monkey mind is to cultivate this awareness within ourselves and integrate the fragmented parts of our psyche. This is the doorway to our infinite potential and genuine happiness.

Let's circle back to the neurological phenomenon, which psychiatrist Edward Hallowell calls attention deficit trait (ADT).[40] This is one of the root reasons you feel overwhelmed and stressed. ADT is our brain's reaction to a hyperkinetic, external environment of speed, data, ideas, and increased workload and the stress of keeping up with all the demands we face. Our high-speed lifestyle requires that our brains track many data points at once—emails, texts, calls, meetings, news, and more—which creates anxiety, hyperactivity, exhaustion, and lack of focus. Here lies the underlying problem—our brains can manage only one task at a time. Technically, our brains switch back and forth from one task to another. When we manage multiple tasks simultaneously it becomes our default mode for working, creating negative physical and mental effects. Research shows that, over time, managing multiple tasks drains our brain's effectiveness and shrinks the gray matter in our neocortex. This causes more mistakes, stress, anxiety, and impatience, as well as stifles our creativity. In addition, it activates our flight-flight-or-freeze stress response. Our brains require rest to recharge and metabolize information while managing the internal biological processes to keep us healthy and resilient.

Although the digital world has revolutionized our ability to connect with people and information globally, it challenges our ability to pay attention, perform at peak levels, and be present with people. One way to determine if you are suffering from ADT is to look at your relationship with your digital devices. Do you find yourself checking your smartphone every moment, whether at work, eating meals, in your car, or walking down the street? When we constantly communicate through our devices, we develop ADT through the addictive behavior of quickly responding or taking action. Hence, we fall into the dopamine trap of instant gratification, from checking off a to-do item to texting a friend. The brain releases dopamine, known as the "feel-good" neurotransmitter, a chemical that exchanges information between neurons. Every time we engage in activities that give us pleasure—like eating, having sex, or getting things done—dopamine gets released. We feel a sense of reward and achievement. Dopamine is essential for happiness and motivation. It's our overindulgence in these activities that causes addictive behavior.

This action-addictive behavior also causes our minds to wander and be less effective. In one Harvard study, Matthew Killingsworth and Daniel Stewart discovered that our minds wander from the actual task at hand 47 percent of the time. The study measured the moods and level of presence of over 5000 people across 83 countries, 86 occupations, and ages 18 to 88. They created an iPhone application to track real-time reports of the thoughts, feelings, and actions of participants engaging in common daily activities such as working, shopping, having sex, bathing, and exercising. They found people's minds wandered least during sex, which is not surprising, and most during grooming activities, like taking a shower. Regardless of whether those in the study had neutral, pleasant, or negative thoughts, they concluded that people were happier when their thoughts were aligned with their emotions and actions while being fully present with one activity at a time.[41] A wandering mind is an unhappy mind. Our minds wander or move into autopilot when we cling to and ruminate about past experiences or worry about or anticipate the future. The researchers discovered that happiness has more to do with the contents of our moment-to-moment experiences than with the major conditions of our lives. Although our minds move into autopilot and get easily distracted, we can train them to be more focused and present in the moment through the mindfulness strategies listed in this chapter.

If our thoughts shape our reality, who creates our thoughts? Our thoughts, or how we perceive the world, are often shaped during early childhood conditioning by our parents, teachers, society, bosses, and even from nongenetic factors through our family lineage as shown in epigenetic research.[42] As you've learned, we formulate an ego or personality structure with a set of beliefs of how we see the world and how to socially interact with others. We learn what is good or bad, right or wrong, safe or dangerous. Often these beliefs are based only on a limited view of the child's experience or their parents' limited belief system and not the complete context of the actual reality. When we experience something, whether good or bad, we generate a thought or perspective about the experience from this narrow view. Our thoughts may generate positive feelings, such as joy, gratitude, and calmness, or negative feelings, such as jealousy, sadness, frustration, anger, or disappointment, depending on our past experience with a similar occurrence. These feelings drive our choices, behaviors, and actions and ultimately create the results we achieve in our careers and lives. When we experience a pleasurable event, we want more of it, and when we experience a negative event, we avoid it at all costs. Rather than learning or healing from the negative experience, we suppress it, which eventually manifests in aggression, hatred, or resentment and hampers our creativity and ability to access our full authentic power. The brain stores memories, both factual and sensational, in the limbic region as early as when we were a baby in our mother's womb. It does this to preserve energy and recall memories or experiences that have the potential to cause us harm. Unfortunately, these negative thoughts and emotions create a vicious cycle and keep us anchored in our past. For example, in your early years, your father may have told you to be quiet at the dinner table with a stern voice that frightened you. You may have internalized this experience as "It's not safe to speak up in front of authority or something bad will happen." Now, as a leader, when your boss speaks to you in a similar stern voice, you may experience the same feelings of inadequacy. This thought can create feelings of shame and not being good enough that get reinforced in the thinking-and-feeling feedback loop in the mind-body neural connections.

Our mind also becomes restless when trying to overcome the common belief of "not being enough." This belief is at the root of our negative mindset and may take the shape of "I am not smart enough, pretty enough, accomplished enough, talented enough, or wealthy enough." We move into overdrive by working harder, not always smarter, to compensate for our feelings of inadequacy or unworthiness. This perpetuates our drive for perfectionism, where we feel we have to do everything perfectly at work or at home to meet unrealistic expectations. We are constantly berating ourselves because we feel like we are not enough.

This false belief is shaped by a limited understanding of who we are as human beings. Based on Eastern philosophy and neuroscience research, who we are is pure consciousness or infinite potential—beyond the ego mind of self-concepts, beliefs, and perceived limitations. As we expand the gray matter in our prefrontal cortex and heart capacities, we can access more innate intelligence, awareness, and loving-kindness beyond our sensory perceptions. Unfortunately, we adopted beliefs from early childhood that shaped our worldview and created the psychological fear of unworthiness. This is simply untrue. We are worthy beyond measure. By always saying yes, not having boundaries, not taking time for self-care, and working hours beyond your physical and mental capacity are examples of how this belief wreaks havoc in our lives. When we do not meet the high expectations we set for ourselves or others, this belief becomes our default mode of thinking and we work harder to prove to others and ourselves that we are worthy. This negative thinking begins looping in our brain chemistry, creating negative states like worry, anger, shame, guilt, fear, and self-doubt. This feeds into the imposter syndrome we experience when we take on a new assignment, new leadership role, or do anything new where we question our ability to do it well and are afraid others may find out that we are a fraud. The fact is, your self-worth and value are not defined by other people's opinions of you. Of course, we all have room to improve our skills to be more masterful and confident at our vocations, but our skills do not define our self-worth. To master the monkey mind, we need to master this self-doubt by embracing our inherent self-value.

This self-doubt gets reinforced by our brain's negativity bias. As Rick Hanson writes in *Rewiring Happiness*, "The mind is like Velcro for negative experiences and Teflon for positive ones."[44] This bias is the central reason we are not experiencing success, happiness, and well-being in our lives. We are constantly looking for what's wrong in our experience versus what's right. I see this pattern with managers and executives all the time. They will receive a performance review from multiple raters—their direct manager, direct reports, and stakeholders—that highlight their strengths, accomplishments, and areas of improvement. Regardless of all the positive feedback received, they remember the negative or constructive feedback. Unfortunately, this demotivates them and often diminishes their performance, especially high achievers. We become fixated with improving the qualities in us we think are flawed rather than focusing on the qualities or strengths in us that make us magnificent.

As we dig a little deeper, we ultimately find we have a fear of failure. This fear can literally stop us in our tracks and discourage us from following our passion and purpose. We may choose complacency and jobs within our comfort zone rather than taking risks and growing to the next level because we fear losing our financial security, being seen as incompetent, or embarrassing our boss or coworkers. This fear of failure is often sourced from a childhood experience or something that didn't go so well at work or school. This may include not getting accepted into an Ivy League school, losing money in the stock market, forgetting key points while presenting at a conference, asserting your viewpoint at a meeting and being shut down by a superior, or leading a large project that costs the company millions of dollars.

When we don't meet our own or other people's expectations, we move into feeling shame or guilt and may vow to never do it again because of the tremendous emotional distress. The superego in action. Psychologists define the difference between shame and guilt as "I am bad" (shame) versus and "I did something bad" (guilt). "I am bad" leads to the false belief of "I am not enough," as discussed above, creating self-judgment and low self-esteem. Shame causes feelings of inadequacy, which in turn make us question our talents and capabilities and block us from experiencing our full potential as a leader and human being.

On the other hand, guilt implies you are a good person who did something bad that can be corrected by an apology and making amends or reparations. It's an inner struggle we all face. It's part of the trials and tribulations on the leader's or hero's journey.

The truth is that every successful leader endures tremendous self-doubt and failure before they experience tremendous success. Basketball legend Michael Jordan says he missed more than nine thousand shots in his career, even several game-winning shots. His ability to fail over and over again is what helped him succeed. Jack Ma, founder and executive chairman of Alibaba, one of the world's largest e-commerce companies, claims he made over one thousand mistakes before he created a multibillion-dollar company. His rags-to-riches story is a testament to his perseverance. From failing college entrance exams, getting rejected by Harvard University ten times, being turned down for thirty jobs, to nearing bankruptcy during the dot.com bubble, he never gave up. His persistence and optimism allowed him to quickly pivot Alibaba's business model to an online export company for buyers globally, which was a game-changing strategy for establishing his multibillion-dollar business. Having a growth and learning mindset rather than a scarcity or fixed mindset will motivate you to embrace lessons of failure and keep moving toward your dreams and goals.

The good news is we can change our negative mindsets. Neuroscience shows we can rewire and create new circuits in our brain through the process of neuroplasticity. Comprising about 2 percent of our body weight, the brain is a complex network of over one hundred billion neurons connected to synaptic structures. These neurons transmit information from electrical impulses to other nerve, muscle, or gland cells. Decades ago, researchers believed that the brain was a static organ that stopped changing after critical developmental periods in childhood; this premise is simply untrue. Magnetic resonance imaging (MRI) has confirmed the brain changes every second and continues to create neural synaptic connections based on habitual patterns.

The brain is malleable and has the ability to reorganize itself, both physically and functionally, throughout our life based on our environment, genetics, behavior, thinking, and emotions. During such changes, the brain engages in synaptic pruning, deleting the neural connections that are no longer necessary or useful and strengthening necessary, useful connections. Every time we recognize a negative thought or habit, reframe it with a positive thought or habit. By engaging in mindful practices such as gratitude, acceptance, and patience, we reprogram our brain to create new neural connections anchored in positive behavioral, thinking, and emotional patterns. As neuropsychologist Donald Hebb says, "Neurons that fire together, wire together."[45] The opposite is also true; neurons that no longer fire together will not wire together. By focusing on our breath through mindfulness meditation practices and not identifying with our emotions and thoughts, we disconnect or unhook from the emotional reactivity from the monkey or unconscious mind. We begin integrating these distorted parts of our human psyche into our essential nature creating coherence and congruence with our reality. This expands our innate intelligence and helps us grow to the next level of our human potential.

Now that you understand the causes and obstacles of the monkey mind and negative thinking, let's explore several mindfulness strategies for cultivating more mastery and mental capacity to overcome and shift these negative mindsets into more positive mindsets.

My Meditation Story

During my mid-twenties, I was stressed and anxious after leaving the family business. Desperately seeking calmness and clarity on my next steps, I attended my first weekend meditation retreat at Idyllwild

Mountains in Southern California. Not knowing what to expect, I drove to the retreat center alone on a Friday afternoon to meet up with a group of meditators. When I arrived at the main cabin, the instructor had meditation zafu cushions laid out in a circle. He shared a dharma talk from the Buddhist teachings and guided us in a meditation practice. There I was, sitting on this uncomfortable cushion in silence, with strangers, and watching my restless mind. Within ten minutes of sitting, my thoughts were racing like wild monkeys. I could not stop the relentless chatter. The meditation lasted for two long hours. I was agitated with all my random thoughts, negative feelings, and the excruciating pain in my legs from sitting cross-legged on the stiff cushion.

Finally, the instructor rang the Tibetan bowl for dinner, which was vegetarian soup and bread. I was relieved—until I discovered the dinner and the rest of the retreat would be held in silence. No talking for three days was a big deal for someone like me who loved conversation. We were assigned roommates and slept in small, rustic cabins with sleeping bags. I barely slept that night. I laid ruminating about my life failures and how to respectfully escape from this retreat. By the next morning, my stress levels had escalated. I packed my belongings and left the retreat early. I drove home and stopped at a fast-food restaurant to self-soothe with a hamburger, fries, and diet cola. I was not ready for meditation, especially sitting in silence for three days.

Three years later, I returned to the meditation practice during graduate school after once again feeling stressed and burned out. This time, I gradually built my physical and mental capacities by practicing hatha yoga to endure sitting for longer periods. Within a few months of yoga and meditation, I started feeling calm, focused, energetic, and more motivated to stay with uncomfortable experiences. For the next twenty years, I studied extensively, committed to the practice, and was finally ready to attend silent retreats with master meditation teachers. I was grateful to learn the tools to master my monkey mind and integrate my emotional reactions. There was much richness in the silence and stillness in the mind. Especially, when I had the patience and awareness that I needed to slow down, relax my body, and observe my inner world with compassion rather than judgment or blame. I now teach mindfulness meditation to people around the world using many of the tools outlined below.

Our deepest calling often shows up mysteriously. Our most challenging experiences invite us to face our fears and break through our perceived limitations. When we move through our fears, we elevate our awareness and mental capacities, which allows us to courageously step into the next level of our potential.

Mindfulness Meditation

Mindfulness meditation is an ancient practice used for quieting the monkey mind. Originating from Hindu and Buddhist traditions and practiced for over five thousand years, meditation is now widely offered as a stress-reduction and mind-training method in corporations and communities around the world. It helps us train our attention and awareness to achieve more mental clarity, emotional balance, and deeper states of relaxation, well-being, and self-realization. To be mindful is to be fully present in the here and now, not ruminating on the past or anticipating or worrying about the future. When we are in a state of mindfulness, we are aware of our thoughts, emotions, and sensations without judgment and as neutral observers. We are able to embrace whatever arises without pushing it away or clinging to the experience.

Jon Kabat-Zinn, psychologist and creator of the mindfulness-based stress-reduction (MBSR) program, says, "Mindfulness is the awareness that arises through paying attention, on purpose, in the present moment, nonjudgmentally in service of self-understanding and wisdom."[46] We essentially become the data scientists of our inner world, which includes our five senses (taste, smell, sound, sight, touch), our body sensations (tightness, tension, temperature), our emotions (pleasant, unpleasant, neutral), and our thoughts (past, present, and future memories or ideas).

Meditation is about bringing a beginner's mind of curiosity and loving-kindness to our inner experience. In doing this, we create space between ourselves and our reactions, uncoupling our conditioned responses from the lower or unevolved regions of the brain. In other words, we're calming or unhooking from the monkey mind's constant chatter. Meditation requires not doing and fully relaxing and letting go, which is counterintuitive to our performance-and-action addiction mindset. It's about "being with" all that arises in the present moment. The challenge we have with being and doing nothing is our fear of letting go of control, not being productive, and facing our insecurities. We have become so enthralled by doing and producing to achieve our goals that we forget about the power of simply being and resting. The good news is that meditation is the doorway to experiencing genuine happiness and our infinite potential, along with providing tremendous work performance and health results. When we finally rest and relax in the present moment, our bodies will naturally return to harmony with our essential nature. Over time and with practice, we begin feeling more joy, love, and appreciation from within rather than seeking these experiences from others. We can meet stressful events and relationships without resistance, having more mental space to respond with awareness and compassion. We become more integrated and grounded in our essence with unshakeable confidence.

Research shows meditation has impressive work-performance and health-related benefits. This includes improved productivity with reduced multitasking,[47] reduced stress,[48] enhanced emotional health,[49] reduced chronic pain,[50] and stabilized healthy blood pressure.[51]

Researchers at Massachusetts General Hospital have found through MRI scans that meditation increases gray matter—the processing neurons—in the prefrontal cortex of our brain. As the meditators expanded their presence, awareness, and compassion, the researchers witnessed decreased emotional reactivity and fight-flight-or-freeze stress response in the lower regions of the brain.

Mindfulness can be practiced in many forms from meditation to everyday activities. We can meditate while sitting, walking, standing, or lying down, where we neutrally observe our direct experience, including our thoughts, emotions, body sensations. We can also practice mindfulness at work and in our everyday life, bringing our full attention and presence to our work or life activities, such as preparing a presentation or washing the dishes, rather than letting our mind wander over past problems or future concerns. Mindfulness can be as simple as pausing, consciously observing your breath during the day, and asking, "Am I present?"

Meditation Practice

There are many types of meditation practices. Whether you are a first-time or seasoned meditator, you'll find the following focused attention meditation to be simple yet effective. It's important to train our minds to be focused and relaxed before moving to advanced meditations such as open awareness. I recommend starting with ten minutes a day and gradually working up to thirty minutes. To successfully create new habits, it's useful to establish a consistent routine. Make a plan for when, how long, and where to practice. For instance, you may prefer practicing early morning, late evening or during a lunch break at home, work, or in nature, for ten minutes. Some researchers suggest practicing meditation in the early morning since your mind is clear, open, creative, and free of distractions, which is a perfect way to set the tone of your day. Find your natural rhythm and customize it to your personal needs. Committing to a daily practice accelerates the benefits while creating new neural pathways to support positive states of mind. If you miss a day or two, simply start again.

1. **Physical space:** Find a quiet, peaceful, clean, and comfortable space where you feel safe, relaxed, and free of any distractions. Turn off any electronic devices.

2. **Body posture:** Sit comfortably with a relaxed, body and tall spine, on a cushion or chair. Place your hands on your lap or thighs, and root your feet on the ground. Gently close your eyes or keep them slightly open with a soft gaze on a single object on the floor. Eyes open helps with mental focus, especially when you feel drowsy.

3. **Breath:** Your breath is your anchor and friend and will help you settle, relax, and calm your mind. Breathe through your nostrils with your attention on your lower abdomen. Observe each inhale and exhale in a noncontrolling and nonengaging way. Become a neutral observer, as if you are watching a movie. Meet your breath as it is without changing it. Notice your breathing without judgment. Is it light or heavy, contracted or expanded, shallow or full? Let the breath breathe you. There is no need to force the breathing pace. It will normalize by itself.

4. **Body scan:** With each inhale, scan your entire body from head to toe for any tension or tightness. With each exhale, relax and release any tension stored in your body. Breathe in and out. Scan your body and release tension. Focus on relaxing and softening your muscles, ligaments, and connective tissues, from your face, neck, shoulders,

and back to your arms, hands, legs, and feet. Letting go of the gripping and tension from the day. With no effort, continue breathing in and out until you feel relaxed and at ease. A relaxed body creates a relaxed, calm mind.

5. **Breath counting:** If your mind is restless and agitated, begin counting from one to ten with every exhale, then backwards from ten to one. Repeat this breathing cycle until your mind is calm. This helps train the mind to focus on a single object rather than wandering from your direct experience or moving into autopilot. If over time your mind is still restless, include a mind-body practice such as yoga or qigong to relax your body and settle your mind before meditating.

6. **Drowsiness:** If you feel drowsy or foggy, there are several techniques you can use to cultivate more mental alertness and activate the sympathetic nervous system: 1) stimulate the breath by breathing deeply through your nose to your lower abdomen; 2) readjust your posture with a tall and relaxed spine; 3) keep your eyes open with a soft gaze on a single object on the ground; and 4) observe your breath and body sensations with a deeper curiosity, maintaining a steady single-pointed focus. Notice where you are breathing in your body and the texture the breath (shallow or full, heavy or light, warm or cool). If you are drowsy after the meditation, this may be a sign you need more restful sleep.

7. **Distractions:** As thoughts, sounds, sensations, and emotions arise, be with them without pushing them away or engaging with them in a dialogue. Simply relax your body and return your focus and attention to your

breath. Labeling the thought, feeling, or body sensation as it arises in your awareness creates more mental space with your experience, especially during discomfort. For example, when you notice your mind thinking constantly about your to-do list, label the thought by silently saying "thinking." When you notice emotions arising such as anger or sadness, label the emotion by silently saying "feeling." When you feel sensations in your body, especially uncomfortable feelings, label the sensations by saying "sensing." Refrain from engaging in your thoughts, emotions, and sensations since this will activate the monkey mind. Simply relax your body and return to your breath. Begin cycling your breath from your nose to your lower abdomen and count, if useful, to regain a stable focus. These distractions will eventually fade away in your experience without your control. Noticing your mind wandering is a good sign—it means you are aware of when your mind moves in autopilot and out of the present moment. When this happens, relax your body and return to your breath without judgment or expectation.

8. **End the practice:** When you're ready to end the practice, gently open your eyes. Take a moment to notice your internal world. See if you can maintain this level of focused attention and presence throughout the day. Write down any insights from the practice.

It's common to face many challenges during meditation such as body tension, restless mind, and drowsiness. The body scanning, focusing on a single object, breath counting, labeling, or stimulating your breath will train your mind to be relaxed, focused and clear in the present moment. Be kind and patient with yourself. Over time, with daily mindfulness training, you will create new neural pathways and cultivate a palpable stillness, aliveness, clarity, and joy.

Harvest the Good Experiences

Research shows that looking for the good in our experiences cultivates inner strengths, such as calm, resilience, compassion, self-worth, and happiness. Try this simple process to begin retraining your mind to reflect, savor, and reframe your negative experiences into positive experiences to create new neural connections:

- **Reflect on the positive experiences from your day.** For example, while presenting to your senior leadership team, you received feedback on how well you stayed composed, confident, and concise when responding to their questions. You may have had moments where you stumbled over your words and forgot important facts. The idea is to anchor on what went well and not dwell on what went wrong. Translate the areas that did not go well into lessons learned for future situations. For example, knowing your leadership team needs more data points on your proposals, you can now build in time to verify and socialize the data, metrics, or facts with a trusted colleague or manager. Over time, this will improve your confidence and communication skills.

- **Savor the positive experience.** Stay with the positive experience for ten to thirty seconds or more. By fully feeling the emotions in your body, such as aliveness or joy, you will intensify those sensations. Focusing on the positive memory activates the dopamine (our feel-good neurotransmitter) in our brain and stores the memory in our limbic region. When we stay with these positive experiences, we create new behaviors that boost our self-esteem, health, and well-being.

- **Reframe the experience.** Review your past experiences and train your mind to look for silver linings and lessons rather than fixating on how circumstances did not work out. Remember, these obstacles on our career path reveal themselves to help you build more capacity and skills to live your destiny with more resilience. For example, if you were not approved for a promotion this year, you may feel discouraged. You may think the system is unfair or that your boss failed to deliver on his promise. Reframe or look for the silver lining in the situation: "It's been a tough quarter financially, and the leadership team has postponed my promotion to help me get ready for the next level. It does not mean anything about my self-worth." This will diminish habitual emotional reactivity and improve your ability to react to difficult situations with equanimity.

Rewrite Your Story

Catherine was a regional sales manager with a stellar track record for exceeding sales targets every quarter. An effective communicator, she was known for building a high-performing team through her compassionate and motivational management style, which empowered her team to perform at their best. However, she received constructive feedback from her manager that she wore her heart on her sleeve, was too emotional, and delayed having the difficult conversations with her team. Catherine was devastated. She started doubting her abilities and wanted to explore ways to lead from a place of compassion and directness without sacrificing her vulnerability and authentic leadership style.

During our coaching engagement, she explored how to build more courage and capacity to have tough conversations and rewrite her current narrative of "It's wrong to be overly sensitive" using the exercise described below. Within a month of practicing this exercise daily, she realized vulnerability is a sign of strength and feedback is a gift. With this growth mindset, she learned to balance her emotional reactions with her rational-thinking mind and respond more appropriately. She also started developing more self-compassion and agency to manage the self-talk that would arise when she did not meet her or others' expectations.

1. To begin this practice, follow the simple mindfulness meditation practice above to get relaxed, focused, and present, breathing fully with each inhale and exhale.

2. Recall a time where you felt not good enough, like a failure, or did not meet your or another person's expectations. Understand that this story may arise from the limited view you had as a child and that as an adult, you can rewrite it with a broader understanding.

3. Ask yourself these questions and observe your responses neutrally. Explore what happens in your body when you believe these thoughts are true and how believing them makes you feel and act:
   • What story am I telling myself?
   • How do I feel when I tell that story?
   • What sensations arise in my body?
   • What evidence or facts tell me that the story is true?
   • Where did this story originate?

4. Mindfully feel any emotions and sensations that may arise to the best of your ability. If too intense, name

them to bring space between your mind and body. Focus on your breathing. Bring compassion to emotions like anger, sadness, or shame rather than criticizing, blaming, or pushing them away. Self-soothe yourself with warmth and tenderness as you would a loved one. Recognize you did your personal best based on your understanding and knowledge at that age and time.

5. Hold your story lightly. Your story is an old mental construct formed by limited information and is not absolute truth or reality. Separate facts from feelings. You can say, "The story I am telling myself is (insert story)". "The truth or fact is that this happened (insert facts), which made me feel (insert feeling)."

6. Create a new story that accurately reflects a broader understanding. Rather than saying "I am not good enough" or "I am a failure," you can shift your story to "I notice I feel nervous and doubt my abilities when I am surrounded by smart or talented people."

7. Reinforce the new story and behaviors, especially when the old story creeps up again. These narratives are built upon many experiences, like the layers of an onion. Creating new thinking and feeling neural pathways requires focus, repetition, and full presence with compassion until it becomes engrained in your cellular memory.

Other Mindful Strategies

Here are other proven mindfulness strategies to help you calm the monkey mind:

- **Take energy breaks:** Research shows that sitting for long periods has negative health effects similar to smoking.[52] Taking breaks every hour allows you to unplug from the busyness of work, move your body, and create mental space for more creativity. This may involve taking a short walk, talking with coworkers or friends, having a healthy meal or drink, or sitting in silence and focusing on your breathing.

- **Create "no-device zones."** Set boundaries for when you use your electronic devices. Turn your phones off and keep them out of reach while eating meals, sleeping, exercising, and spending time with family and friends. Turn off Wi-Fi at night. Research shows that when you unplug from digital screens two hours before bed and go to sleep before 10:30 p.m., your melatonin levels increase and your sleep quality is improved.

- **Turn notifications off.** Media applications, including Facebook, Instagram, Gmail, and Twitter, send alerts on new posts and messages. To avoid being bombarded with alerts, turn them off and set a specific time to check your messages. These alerts stimulate a fight-flight-or-freeze response, shifting our attention to move into action.

- **Connect with nature.** As noted earlier, nature is pure medicine for regulating our nervous system. Its grounding properties support relaxation and enhance oxygen levels and well-being. Schedule time to go outside; walk in your neighborhood or hike along the coast or in the forest. You will feel nourished and ready to reengage in work.

- **Move your body.** Physical exercise, such as running, vigorous yoga (vinyasa or ashtanga), or walking can regulate heart rate, improve circulation, burn off stress, and increase endorphins (the "happy hormone"). For those needing to slow down, qigong, yin, or restorative yoga can help regulate stress hormones, calm the busy mind, and enhance overall well-being. See Key #3.

- **Do a digital fast.** Go device-free. Do a digital fast from social media, texting, online videos, and all electronics. Engage in mindfulness meditation and activities that bring you deep nourishment and joy, such as a weekend getaway, meditation retreat, creative project, playing an instrument, or a digital-free hobby.

- **Journal:** For about fifteen minutes without stopping, write down what you are thinking, feeling, and worrying about. Let your monkey mind run wild. Don't hold back. When we write down our thoughts, complaints, and insecurities, we settle our minds. We can identify common patterns and address challenges with more objectivity and resilience. Apply your insights to your everyday life.

Now that you understand how to master the monkey mind, we will explore how to build emotional resilience and a courageous heart during stressful and challenging situations.

Reflections

- What fears or negative mindsets are keeping you from achieving your dreams? What is the story you are telling yourself? What evidence from your past or present make this true?
- What are the silver linings and learnings from your negative or stressful experiences?
- What is an empowering mindset or narrative that can inspire you to achieve your goals?
- Which of the mindfulness strategies above will help you stay focused, calm, and productive?
- Meditation Challenge: Commit to a daily mediation practice for at least ten minutes for the next thirty days.

KEY #5

Grow a Resilient and Courageous Heart

*Resilience is about adapting to challenging times and having the
courage to persevere with a brave heart, even when you want to
give up.*

Sarita was an emerging leader working on a technology collaboration team. She was strategic, energetic, loyal, emotionally intelligent and known for her authenticity, direct communication, and getting things done. Her direct communication style was her superpower. It helped her influence senior leaders and stakeholders to drive her projects with ease and impact. However, some coworkers or internal stakeholders found her style too controlling and demanding—making it challenging for Sarita to get their commitment on key initiatives.

In leading one critical project, Sarita had an intense, high-stakes conversation about the deployment schedule with a coworker, which brought up strong emotions and insecurities in her. Instinctually, she pulled away and avoided this person for a while and spent days ruminating about what she did to upset him. During a coaching call, we explored the situation and her emotional triggers in depth. We discussed how she might have more courageous conversations that created win-win outcomes using skills such as empathy, active listening, and asking questions to better understand her coworker's viewpoint. Sarita spent years developing the emotional capacity to investigate her triggers through books, practice, and therapy. She was committed to doing the inner work. With thoughtful reflection and consistent practice, she became more skilled at regulating her emotional reactions. This gave her the confidence and courage to follow up with her coworker, listen to his concerns, and negotiate timelines.

In this chapter, we will explore the fifth key, *Grow a Resilient and Courageous Heart*. This key allows us to increase our emotional intelligence, resilience, and courage in navigating stressful high-stakes situations, challenging relationships, and uncertain times. The previous chapter provided the tools we need to master the monkey mind. This is foundational for building more capacity and resilience to dive deeper into the emotional centers of the brain and heart.

Building Emotional Intelligence and Resilience

Emotional intelligence (EI) is a key ingredient of great leadership and being resilient at work and in life. According to Travis Bradberry, EI is our "ability to recognize and understand emotions in ourselves and others, and the ability to use this awareness to manage your behavior and relationships."[53] Accounting for 58 percent of performance in all types of jobs, it's the single biggest predictor of performance in the workplace and the strongest driver of leadership and personal excellence. Additionally, people with high EI make more money—an average of $29,000 more per year than people with low EI. There are many key thought leaders in the field of emotional intelligence, from psychologist Daniel Goleman, who popularized EI in the USA, to psychologist Travis Bradberry, author of Emotional Intelligence 2.0. We will explore the time-tested strategies of these EI thought leaders, along with best practices from my empirical research working with leaders. We will investigate how to develop four EI core competencies—self-awareness, self-management, social awareness, and relationship management—to strengthen our relationships with ourselves and others.

Self-Awareness

Self-awareness is the ability to understand our own emotions and their effects on our performance and relationships. Building self-awareness requires getting clear about our strengths, weaknesses, and values (see Key #1), about what situations or people push our buttons, about how we feel, and about how our emotions may impact others. Bradberry explains that all emotions are derivatives of five core feelings: happiness, sadness, anger, fear, and shame. As neuroscience research has shown, negative emotions are triggered by people and experiences we perceive may threaten our safety. Our physiological reaction is the same whether we face a truly life-threatening situation or something as mundane as not meeting a project deadline. The good news is, we can control our thoughts and reactions to our emotions as long as we are aware of them in the moment. In the workplace, we are often conditioned not to express our emotions. There is pressure to be more rational and objective with our decisions and how we lead our teams. However, in today's VUCA world, it's important to show up more human, vulnerable, rational, empathetic, and transparent when leading teams or navigating a global crisis like the 2020 pandemic. EI skills are more critical than ever to ensure leaders show up calm, resilient, confident, positive, empathetic, and courageous in leading change. There are many other work activities that require us to manage our emotions, such as giving and receiving feedback, meeting tight deadlines, dealing with challenging relationships, working with limited resources to drive our priorities, and enduring setbacks and failures. Our emotions serve a purpose and are simply reactions to our external world. Often signaling us to investigate what is important to us and how to communicate our needs more explicitly. It's easy to manage emotions when they are positive, such as joy and excitement, but when it comes to negative emotions, it requires more self-reflection to avoid doing something we may regret, such as yelling at our boss, team, or significant other during a disagreement. Experiment with the following three strategies to cultivate more self-awareness.

Observe your emotions. Capture your thoughts and emotions in a daily journal. Reflect on your day, exploring these questions: 1) what went well? 2) what was challenging? 3) how did I feel? and 4) how did I respond? Without judgment, write down which situations or people made you feel happy, excited, and alive, and which ones made you feel angry, disappointed, and frustrated. Write the physical sensations you felt in your body during those situations. These sensations might include tight muscles, a clenched jaw, a fast heart rate, sweating, tingling, pacing, and twitching. Notice if you had a tendency to fight (argue, attack, or get defensive), flee (move away, mask, or avoid) or freeze (shut down or stutter). When we write down our emotions, it helps us step outside our emotional reactivity and allows us to build more objectivity and self-compassion. In Sarita's case, she needed to move away from the situation to further reflect on her feelings and the dynamics of the relationship with her colleague. This space allowed her to process her strong emotions, dissect her triggers, and respond more objectively. Once she investigated her reactions, she was able to achieve project deadlines more collaboratively.

Know your triggers. Triggers are experiences or people who push your buttons and cause strong emotional reactivity. It's our amygdala hijack in action. To understand these triggers, I suggest getting a notepad and drawing three vertical columns. In the first column, list the situations and people that trigger or frustrate you. This may include people who are lazy, stupid, selfish, arrogant, critical, or low performers, or situations where you were not informed about a critical business decision or were micromanaged or controlled by your boss. In the second column, write your stress response and emotional reaction. For example, did you shut down, fight, or run away? Were you angry, frustrated, hurt, or disappointed? In the third column, write a time when this happened in the past, whether in childhood or during your career. This may be when your boss gave you critical feedback and you felt insecure and hurt, like when your mother criticized you about talking too much or doing certain activities the wrong way.

Integrate your emotional reactions. Once you build more awareness of your triggers and emotional reactions, the next step is to feel and integrate your emotions to build emotional resilience. Often, the emotions that show up in our life are unresolved issues from the past that will plague us until they are understood, healed, and integrated into our mind and body. It's similar to uninstalling old software in your computer's hard drive. You need to remove the old software application to upgrade to the new program.

Before processing these emotions, I invite you to find a place in your body that feels grounded and strong, or an external place you go that feels safe, happy, and peaceful, like the forest or beach. This is your resource for building emotional capacity. Now, from this place, lean into the discomfort and feel the emotional reaction (anger, jealousy, frustration, disappointment, sadness, etc.). The brain will naturally trigger physical sensations in your body (heart rate racing, breath quickening, palms sweating). This fight-flight-or-freeze response is triggered by the amygdala, or emotional brain. As sensations and emotions arise, breathe in and out, deep inside your lower abdomen and be with the discomfort without resisting it. Your emotions will run their natural course and integrate into the emotional brain. It's important to stay with the emotion as if you were holding a small infant you love dearly. This is the art of rewiring your negative mindsets and creating more positive states of mind. If the emotion becomes too overwhelming, disconnect from it and return to your resource, or happy place, and attend to the emotion later, when you feel stronger.

Seeking guidance from a trained coach or therapist is recommended and important when working with deep-rooted emotional or traumatic experiences. Know that anytime you feel anger or other strong emotions, you can slow down, take a deep breath, step back from the situation, and examine what your emotions or physical sensations may be telling you. With practice, it will get easier, and you will have more emotional resiliency when faced with challenging and uncertain situations.

Self-Management

Self-management is the ability to use our awareness of emotions to stay flexible and act positively when engaging with another person or situation. When we skillfully manage our emotional reactions, making rushed decisions, compromising our values, or judging others for their behaviors, we cultivate more impulse control. This allows us to address the situation objectively and take more personal accountability for our actions and mistakes. Here are three strategies for regulating your emotions.

Be calm under pressure. Your breath is your best friend and anchor during times of stress. As strong emotions, such as anger and frustration, arise, begin breathing deeply from your diaphragm and feel your feet rooted on the ground. Diaphragmatic breathing floods the brain with oxygen, while shallow breathing causes poor concentration, anxiousness, mood swings, and low energy. If your breathing does not relax your emotional reactivity, begin counting from one to ten with every exhale and then backward from ten to one, cycling the breath until you feel more relaxed. This will activate the parasympathetic nervous system, as discussed in Key #3, and will shift your body from the fight-flight-or-freeze stress response into a relaxed, calm state. Oxygen in the brain allows the prefrontal cortex, the brain's rational center, to dismantle the emotional reactivity for you to meet the situation with more objectivity, flexibility, and creativity.

Reframe your negative self-talk. "According to the National Science Foundation, the average person has about 12,000 to 60,000 thoughts per day. Of those, 80 percent are negative, and 95 percent are repetitive."[54] The strong relationship between what you think, feel, and behave is part of your neural connections. Our thoughts can create our reality if we become attached to them and believe they are true. Most of the time, as we've learned, our thoughts are often a distortion of the actual experience. We have the capacity to regulate our thinking mind through consistent practice of mindfulness meditation and understanding and changing our negative self-talk. To change your negative self-talk, try these three strategies:

- Avoid absolute language, like always and never; instead, use words like sometimes or this time.
- Reframe your harsh judgments, like "I am such an idiot. I should have known better" to "I am learning, and I made a mistake." Separating facts from judgments or feelings makes room for more objectivity, self-compassion, and understanding of a situation.
- Take personal responsibility for your part in the situation and avoid blaming others or taking on the entire burden.

Recharge your mind and body. Take time for self-reflection, problem-solving, restful sleep, and meditation. When you give yourself space from a challenging situation, it allows you to calm down, process your emotions, and gain a fresh perspective. You may be pleasantly surprised to find important lessons and silver linings that emerge from that challenging situation and open you to a new way of working, thinking, and being in the world. For example, when shelter-in-place occurred, I was frustrated that I could not do my normal routine of yoga, travel, spend time with friends without a mask, and hike in the redwoods. But isolating in my home for many months made me realize I needed to slow down, sleep more, declutter my home, and realign my work and life priorities.

Social Awareness

Social awareness is the ability to accurately observe other people's emotions and better understand what is going on in a situation. It involves perceiving what other people are thinking and feeling by observing body language and other cues. To do this, we need to pause, stop talking, stop the self-talk running through our minds, stop anticipating what the other person is going to say, and stop planning a response. We listen actively, observe attentively, and hold space for the other person to talk without interruption. This helps us see the whole picture, unhook from our emotional reactions, and thoughtfully respond to the situation in a timely manner. To build social awareness, try these two powerful strategies.

Be present. Being present means not reflecting on the past or planning for the future; it means being fully present in this moment, in the here and now. As Eckart Tolle, author of *Power of Now*, says, "Realize deeply that the present moment is all you have. Make the now the primary focus of your life."[55] This means not multitasking, interrupting the other person, or planning a clever response. Being in the present moment is about listening to the other person with curiosity and suspending biases and judgments. You may be surprised what you learn about the other person without imposing your own assumptions, opinions, and reactions.

Be empathetic. Empathy is about putting yourself in someone else's shoes. It helps when developing the people on your team, challenging opposing views, giving constructive feedback, and listening to those in need. By putting ourselves in someone else's position, we can lean in, ask questions, understand their viewpoint, and find ways to forge a stronger relationship. Our body language and intonation also play an integral role in demonstrating empathy. Research shows that body language and intonation account for 93 percent of our communication, while words account for only 7 percent. Body language can show up as arms crossed, eyes averted, nodding, pacing, smiling, and various facial expressions. While intonation shows up in the tone, volume, and tempo of what you or the other person are saying. These cues inform you of the words or feelings not being spoken by the other person. This helps determine how to respond appropriately. When leading with empathy, it's helpful to listen, ask questions and speak congruently, ensuring your nonverbal cues match your actual words.

Relationship Management

Relationship management is the ability to be aware of our own emotions as well as the emotions of others to manage interactions effectively. This requires clear communication, skillful handling of conflict, and taking the time to build trusting relationships. Our interpersonal skills and ability to cultivate strong relationships are essential in getting things done, influencing people to commit to our mission, debating ideas about a decision or project, and moving to the next level of leadership.

Below are three key strategies for building strong relationships and clear communication.

Create win-win outcomes. We all have times when we don't see eye to eye with someone. When stakes are high, emotions are strong, and viewpoints are conflicting, we have what is called a "crucial conversation." Building upon the research in the Joseph Grenny and team's book, *Crucial Conversations*, and my client-work experience, I developed the following process for facilitating courageous conversations to build awareness, trust, and healthy dialogue that lead to win-win outcomes.

Before the conversation: Examine the situation by exploring these questions:

- Why does the situation require a courageous conversation?
- What is your stress response: are you fleeing (masking, avoiding, withdrawing), fighting (controlling, labeling, or attacking) or freezing (shutting down)? For example, when my manager gave me constructive feedback, I got defensive, moved to attacking, and cited examples where I thought he was wrong or inaccurate.
- What are the implications or costs of not addressing the situation?
- What are your thoughts, assumptions, and feelings about the person or situation?
- What facts, behaviors, or evidence make this true?
- What do you want or need for yourself and the other person?

Journal Prompt: Based on this (challenging situation), I reacted by (fighting, fleeing, or freezing). This showed up as (behaviors). The costs of not addressing this situation are (insert). My thoughts and assumptions are (insert). This situation made me feel (insert). The facts and evidence that make this true are (behavioral observations or facts). What I want or need for me is (insert). What I want or need for this person is (insert).

During the conversation: Leverage the following guidelines.

- Suspend judgment, be empathetic, and listen to the other person's viewpoint.
- Own your experience and avoid blaming or finger-pointing.
- Share your appreciation for the person to build mutual respect, and frame the conversation to align with a common purpose.
- Share your observations and needs in behavioral terms with facts and how the situation impacted you.
- Explore the other person's side of the story by listening to his or her perspective in a neutral and unbiased way.
- Reinforce where you agree and identify the areas where you disagree.
- Explore options or strategies to create a win-win solution.
- Agree on next steps and thank the person for engaging in the conversation.

Conversation Prompt: Thanks for being available for this meeting. My intent is to share some observations about the (situation). First, I appreciate that we are (common purpose). This is my view of the situation (facts, evidence, behavioral observations). I felt (feeling) by your (person's response or action). What I need from you is (insert). What I want for us is (insert). I am curious about your perspective about (situation). Now, listen actively to the other person's story. Explore options, identify where you disagree, and find ways to create a win-win solution. Tailor your conversation to your authentic communication style.

Deliver clear communication. Effective communication is vital to earning trust with your team, management, customers, and stakeholders. It includes active listening; asking questions; speaking clearly, concisely, and appropriately; and responding to questions. Have a beginner's mindset by being open and curious about the other person's viewpoint as if it is the first time you've heard it. Explain the rationale ("why") behind key decisions and lead by example, ensuring your intentions align with your actions. Mixed signals often burn bridges quickly. Provide a positive, transparent, and concise set of messages that supports your team through uncertainty and change. Ensure that your words are aligned with your energy, tone, and body language to avoid your message being misunderstood. Other factors for effective communication include showing you care by acknowledging the other person's feelings and building agreement on how best to work collaboratively in the future.

Give clear, constructive feedback. Giving constructive feedback is one of the most difficult activities for a leader or anyone in general. It brings up tremendous worry, procrastination, and fear of hurting another person. It also activates the person receiving the feedback into a stress response and the negative mindset of "Who I am is not good enough" and "I need to be fixed." Many leaders have found it useful to reframe the feedback as a gift or service to help team members grow and succeed in their careers.

Buckingham and Goodall's book, *Nine Lies about Work*, offers a strengths-based approach for giving feedback that motivates people to grow to the next level of excellence rather than diminishing their self-esteem. Additionally, I've found that a balanced approach helps people not only understand what they did well but also areas for growth that would elevate their performance. When giving feedback, it's best to focus on specific behaviors or observations as opposed to judgments about the person. Imposing your biases and judgments diminishes the other person rather than motivating or challenging them to thrive and excel. As the old adage goes, "When you fish for a person, they can only eat for the day; when you teach them to fish, they can eat for a lifetime." Similarly, giving feedback with a coaching mindset encourages team members to learn, grow, make mistakes, and achieve more sustainable performance over time. Try the following approach for giving feedback to your team member:

- Explore the situation from the other's perspective.
  - What worked well? What did not work well?
  - How have you handled this situation in the past?
  - What do you want to see happen in the future?
- Share what worked well from your perspective.
  - When you did (insert), here are two-three things that worked for me (in behavioral terms), and here's why. For example, when you delivered the presentation, I observed you being prepared with a clear business case for your proposed solution, responding to challenging questions with specific answers, and providing next steps for your audience to take action.
- Share observations that may be blind spots or upgrades to the person's performance.
  - When you did (insert), I experienced (state two or three observations). For example, when you delivered that presentation, I experienced

you getting too much into the details, not listening to cues, and getting defensive when people challenged your ideas. What was showing up for you during that time?

- Be present, silent, empathetic, and listen to the other's perspective without judgment. It's natural for people to get defensive and have strong reactions. The self-management skills we've discussed will keep you centered, neutral, and objective.

- Agree on a path forward to practice the new behaviors while motivating the person to excel with more confidence.

- Follow up with the team member in regular one-on-one meetings to acknowledge, praise, reinforce, and share any specific observations.

Growing a Courageous Heart

In March 2017, I received a call—the call you never want to receive. My brother asked me to fly over to visit my mother soon because my mom's health had declined dramatically. She was given a prognosis of pulmonary fibrosis (lung disease) and advanced type 2 diabetes with only two months to live. My heart dropped instantly, and a force of compassion came through me like a lightning bolt, propelling me to take action. I flew down to visit my parents and was devastated to see my mother lifeless, staring at the wall, sedated with medications, and on oxygen. This was a woman who had eight children, seventeen grandchildren, a heart of gold, and tremendous courage and energy in the face of adversity. I held my mother's pale hands and looked into her tired brown eyes. She leaned over and whispered, "Help me!" Without hesitation, I leaped into action.

Having experienced my own health challenges, I contacted my naturopathic doctor in town and was fortunate to get an appointment from a last-minute cancellation. I called my brother for help, and we drove my mom to see the doctor. He conducted some diagnostic tests and recommended a specific diet and nutritional supplement program to best support her health. We implemented the health protocol when we got home, and within forty-eight hours, my mom regained her spirit and energy and was able to communicate with us again. With support from my family, we rallied together, changed my mother's diet, and got her off all medications except insulin. We leveraged nutritional supplements and the latest health research for reversing diabetes. Three years later, at eighty-six, she engages at family gatherings, and her physical health and well-being had significantly improved.

Building a foundation of emotional intelligence through self-awareness, self-management, social awareness, and relationship management allows us to move deeper into cultivating a more resilient and courageous heart. Courage is the mental or moral strength to persevere in the face of danger, fear, and difficulty. Research shows we have the ability to grow inner strengths to create a happy and productive life. As we practice and apply these EI skills, we can reduce emotional reactivity and stress, heal psychological wounds, and improve resilience, well-being, and life satisfaction.[56]

Research conducted by the Heartmath Institute shows that when we express or sense positive emotional states, it creates normal-variability heart rates, sending a coherent heart rhythm pattern to the brain, which activates the autonomic nervous system. During stress and negative emotional states, the heart's rhythm pattern is erratic and disordered, inhibiting higher cognitive functions like the ability to think clearly, learn, reason, and make effective decisions.[57]

This study correlates with Dr. Armour's research in 1991, where he discovered the heart has a little brain or "intrinsic cardiac nervous system." Comprised of over 40,000 neurons, our heart brain acts independently of the cranial brain and generates the largest electromagnetic field in the body. As it receives information from our internal and external environment, it sends messages to the brain through the limbic and neocortex regions. This feedback loop helps modulate feelings of pain or pleasure as well as helps us learn, remember, make decisions, and access intuition.[58]

In this section, you will learn five inner strengths to cultivate more courage in the face of challenge, adversity, and uncertainty. These strengths or heart capacities are gratitude, loving-kindness, compassion, sympathetic joy, and equanimity. They are widely researched in the field of psychology and neuroscience and revered in spiritual traditions such as Buddhism and Hinduism for thousands of years. They have the power to nourish a broken heart, calm an overactive mind, and transform negative habitual thinking patterns from our conditioned mind.

Gratitude is about having a deep appreciation for the goodness and lessons in our lives and for the kind and generous offerings of others. From ancient practices to modern research, gratitude has been shown to be a transformational power when it comes to our physical health and well-being. Research shows that gratitude reduces depression, PTSD incidents, and toxic emotions such as envy and resentment while improving our mood, personal resilience, interpersonal relationships, and well-being.[59] Moreover, writing in a gratitude journal or expressing gratitude creates physical benefits such as reduced physical pain and chronic fatigue, improved sleep, and increased cardiac function.[60] Gratitude helps us shift negative mindsets by reframing our interpretations, looking for what was right or good in a situation, accepting what we already have, and applying our positive habits to achieve our goals.[61]

For example, Stephanie, a high-powered executive leading a billion-dollar business, was having a hard time accepting the negative feedback her peers gave her during a 360-performance review. The feedback haunted her. She felt insecure about her capabilities and a relentless fear that she would be branded by their perceptions, impacting her next promotion. I suggested she start a daily gratitude practice documenting three things she was grateful for and all the positive experiences of her day. Within several months, something miraculous happened. She stopped worrying about others' perceptions and started acknowledging her unique strengths and embracing her imperfections. She began exuding more presence and happiness with her work and relationships.

Loving-kindness is a tender and benevolent affection toward others, given without expectations. Have you noticed that it's hard to be kind to challenging people? When we are overly critical of others (or even ourselves) for making mistakes, not showing up ethically, or not meeting expectations, we guard our hearts, inhibiting us from feeling loving-kindness. This pattern (often sourced from painful childhood experiences) will create negative thoughts or narratives that are deeply programmed in our brain chemistry.

Unfortunately, the more we judge ourselves, the more we are inclined to project our fears, judgments, and insecurities onto our significant partners, friends, or colleagues. By developing loving-kindness through self-inquiry and meditation, our hearts soften and our defense mechanisms eventually dissolve. We begin trusting and treating ourselves with more warmth, tenderness, and kindness. We take on the view and understanding that "everyone wants to be happy." Over time, we become aware of our emotional triggers, embrace our experiences as a gift for learning, and have more space to love without expectation. We communicate our needs more clearly, make time for self-care, and realize that everyone is experiencing some level of pain and suffering. For example, Jonathan, a brilliant engineer, was on the promotion path to be a director. He was a sincere, friendly, savvy leader who always strived to do the right thing for his team and business. Jonathan expected himself to perform at peak levels and had an unwavering drive for excellence. At times, he was self-critical when he did not meet his or others' expectations. I asked him, "What would it look like if you were kind to yourself right now?" He paused and, in that moment, noticed his inner critic in action. With this new realization, he consciously started being more kind to himself. Whenever he found himself engaging in negative self-talk, he stopped and shifted to being more positive and forgiving when he didn't meet his expectations. By being kind to himself, he had more capacity to be more kind and patient with others when they struggled to meet work expectations.

Compassion is the ability to meet our own and others' pain and suffering with an open heart. Cultivating loving-kindness paves the way for us to be compassionate to ourselves and others. Compassion is different than empathy in that you not only have the capacity to connect with another person's challenges or pain, you have a deep desire to do something to help them. I learned the art of compassion from my own and my mother's healing journeys. As mentioned previously, in my early thirties, when I was diagnosed with chronic fatigue syndrome, I felt shame and sadness that my body was struggling while my friends were healthy and pursuing their dreams. Inevitably, my pain became my purpose, motivating me to study nutrition, psychology, neuroscience, yoga, and meditation to better understand the healing power of my body, heart, and mind intelligences. Through healthy lifestyle changes, consistent yoga and meditation practice, and support from holistic health practitioners, I transformed my health and developed immense compassion for those who face difficult hardships. This was useful when my mother began to struggle with health challenges. A force of love and compassion propelled me to take positive action. I was able to engage and educate other family members to help my mother make changes that ultimately saved her life. When we can meet our own suffering with acceptance, compassion, and understanding, we can hold space for the suffering of others, creating miracles for deeper connection, love, and transformation.

Sympathetic joy is the ability to be happy for and delight in the success of others. When we have compassion, we can more easily celebrate others' joys, such as a loving marriage, successful career, job promotion, financial freedom, or vibrant health. However, when we are in a state of suffering or dissatisfaction, we are more likely to be afflicted with jealousy, anger, or aversion. We start comparing ourselves with our peers, family members, or friends, which perpetuates our feeling of unworthiness and also separates us from fully celebrating the success or fortune of people we care about. I have often witnessed this kind of comparing with my coaching clients, especially when promotions are granted to specific individuals that may not have the depth of the qualifications and experience my clients do. This ultimately leads to resentment toward their peers and leadership team. They may believe the promotion process is unfair: promoting unqualified people or using a process that is inconsistent across teams.

While this may be true, we may not see the bigger picture or completely understand the reasons behind a certain decision. In these situations, explore what's in your control and what's out of your control. Take action for the situations in your control and find the courage to accept or explore ways to influence the situations out of your control. This might include having a courageous conversation to express your concerns to avoid harboring resentment or passive aggression toward another person. The doors we are meant to walk through will open, while the doors we were not meant to walk through will close. This is where we trust that something bigger than us is leading us to our destiny.

Cultivating sympathetic joy sounds simple, but is not easy. It requires the cultivation of our character, feeling gratitude for what we already have, embracing our imperfections, and accepting and letting go of situations out of our control. We begin trusting that another opportunity will show up and proactively taking action toward goals that bring greater success and fulfillment. This restores our generosity and inherent capacity to experience joy for others' happiness and success.

Equanimity is the ability to be with our experience without clinging to it or pulling away from it. It requires stepping away from a situation that pushes our buttons and observing our reactivity with sincere honesty. No matter what arises, we meet life with an open, responsive, and balanced heart and mind. We let go of aversion or attachment to a specific outcome, and we accept what is without feeling the need to control or change the situation. This invites us to experience our fear, frustration, sadness, pain, and joy with more spaciousness and stillness rather than suppression and aggression. A balanced heart doesn't mean we don't feel pleasure or pain; it means staying open, neutral, and patient, as well as holding our emotions with tenderness and compassion without labeling them as good or bad. By developing equanimity, we build the capacity to be with our vulnerability and reactivity without judgment. We communicate with more courage and take responsibility for creating genuine happiness and fulfillment in our lives, careers, and relationships.

When we emanate these inner strengths, we have a positive influence on our teams, family, and communities. Over the last two decades, scientists have discovered we have a special class of brain cells that get activated when a person observes someone else's physiological or emotional state. Italian scientists, Giacomo Rizzaolatti and Vittorio Gallese, call these mirror neurons. In a research study, they measured the brain activity of monkeys during different motor activities. When one of the researchers reached out for food, they noticed the monkeys would mimic the same action. They cited that the motor command neurons in the prefrontal cortex would fire within the person doing the action as well as with the monkey or person watching the action. They also discovered when a person experiences an emotion, such as sadness or anger, neurons in the insular cortex of the brain begin to fire. If someone witnesses the pain, they will begin to empathize with the other person's pain. Professor of neuroscience V.S. Ramachadran asserts: "Mirror neurons will do for psychology what DNA did for biology—and open a whole new field of investigation."[62]

These mirror neurons have a profound effect in creating a positive culture in business. When we, as leaders, show up with gratitude, loving-kindness, compassion, and equanimity with our teams and colleagues, they will naturally emulate these positive behaviors. Our behaviors set the tone of our team culture. Leaders who embody these qualities will most likely build teams that are more engaged, creative, and happy at work. I witnessed this first-hand with my coaching clients. Leaders with high EI skills will often receive higher team engagement scores than leaders with lower EI skills, specifically around psychological safety and trust. Growing a resilient and courageous heart will not only enhance your health and well-being, but will also elevate your impact as a leader. People follow leaders who are honest, trustworthy, compassionate, and who champion their success.

To cultivate these inner strengths and enrich your career and life, experiment with these six practices on a consistent basis:

1. **Keep a gratitude journal.** Create a ritual of writing down at least three things you are grateful for each day. On days where you feel demotivated or are having a bad

day, read through your journal and breathe in all the things, experiences, and people that are good in your life. This will help shift our negative biases to positive states of mind. It builds more resilience to not give up even after our toughest days.

2. **Count your blessings.** Take time to reflect on your life and recall the blessings you've received from others or a higher power. You may be grateful for vibrant health, a thriving career or the financial abundance to buy a beautiful home, traveling across the globe, or being able to donate to your favorite charity. Also, take time to reflect on your hardships or challenges, such as divorce, job loss, or illness, and identify the blessing or gift of each experience. This will help train your brain to assign a more positive outlook on negative experiences and transmute regrets and resentments into wisdom, gratefulness, and the motivation to achieve your dreams.

3. **Express your appreciation.** Think about the people who've impacted your life in a positive way. This may be your family, for their unconditional support; your team, for the excellence they deliver to your customers; or your gardener, who makes your home look beautiful. Write a thank-you note, surprise them with a gift, or call them to express your gratitude and appreciation. This will open your heart as well as strengthen your relationships.

4. **Engage in random acts of kindness.** Have you ever received an unexpected gift or kind gesture from someone? I remember driving through a toll bridge in Northern California only to find that a stranger had already paid for my fee. Although it happened years ago, I'm still

grateful for this person's generosity. Find creative ways to randomly express kindness to your neighbors, to strangers, or to the people who support you throughout the year, like your gardener or health practitioner.

5. **Practice radical acceptance.** During challenging times, we may feel helpless, frustrated, worried, and anxious. We may not know how to manage our life or global circumstances. A useful mindful—and business prioritization—practice is to assess which things are in your control and which are out of your control. For those things within your control, write down what action you can take to resolve the situation. For those things out of your control, let go of the worry or find a way to influence and make the situation better. If it's difficult to let go of the situation and move on, it means you have some level of resistance to the situation. When this happens, leverage this radical acceptance practice:

- Bring your awareness to the thought or emotion arising. Notice the resistance.
- Be with the emotion without pushing it away or engaging with it. You can label your emotions to give space to the reactivity such as: this feeling is anger, fear, disappointment, worry, or frustration.
- Breathe in an out to relax the body until the emotional reactivity diffuses.
- Avoid judging yourself and accept your reality with compassion and radical acceptance.
- If you cannot move forward, notice if there is an action you can take to resolve the situa-

tion. You may need to do this practice multiple times until you feel peace in your heart or work with a qualified coach or therapist.

6. **Loving-kindness meditation:** A transformative way to cultivate a kind, grateful and compassionate heart is to practice the loving-kindness meditation. Loving-kindness is an unconditional love you give yourself or someone without expectations or conditions. To get started, gently close your eyes and sit with a straight, relaxed back and body. Begin breathing in and out from your heart center without controlling your breath. When you're attuned to the loving and warm energy in your heart, slowly recite the following phrases, with intention and compassion, as if you or the person was sitting in front of you. Start with yourself, followed by a person you love, a neutral person, a challenging person, and, finally, all human beings:

   - *To yourself:* "May I be happy. May I be healthy. May I be free from suffering. May I have peace in my heart."
   - *To someone you love:* "May you be happy. May you be healthy. May you be free from suffering. May you have peace in your heart."
   - *To someone neutral:* "May you be happy. May you be healthy. May you be free from suffering. May you have peace in your heart."
   - *To someone challenging:* "May you be happy. May you be healthy. May you be free from suffering. May you have peace in your heart."

- *To all human beings:* "May all beings be happy. May all beings be healthy. May all beings be free from suffering. May all beings have peace in their hearts."

Now that you understand the art and science of building emotional resilience and a courageous heart in navigating challenging relationships and situations, we will explore how to bring your most powerful and authentic self to your work with more courage and confidence.

Reflections

- What skills would help you build more emotional intelligence and resilience?
- What inner strengths would help you build a more courageous heart?

KEY #6
Be Your Authentic Self

When we embrace our perfections and imperfections, we build more confidence and trust our inner wisdom rather than seeking the validation of others for our worth and value.

Venkat led a team that delivered education solutions to internal customers in a multinational technology company. He was enthusiastic, ambitious, and compassionate who had a strong reputation as a learning expert leading large-scale learning initiatives and built high-performing teams. As Venkat's work scope, team, and visibility increased, he was asked to present his team's work to executive leaders across multiple business functions.

As someone who led from behind the scenes, Venkat had tremendous trepidation about public speaking, especially in front of high-powered executives. On stage, he would experience stress and anxiety, which showed up as speaking too fast, fidgeting with his hands, or not connecting with his audience. During our coaching engagement, Venkat wanted to learn the art of leadership presence and delivering impactful presentations using storytelling. He often compared himself with others he admired: "I want to be calm, articulate, and engaging, like top leaders." I challenged him to think about how he might show up as his powerful and authentic self. In astonishment, he paused and said with clarity, "Yes, that is who I want to be." After three short months, applying best practices in executive presence, communications, and mindfulness, Venkat started receiving positive feedback from senior leaders and his peers. They commented about his calm presence, clear and concise message, and how genuine he was in delivering his presentations. Venkat realized the key to his speaking success was being his authentic self.

Authenticity is about presence, living in the moment with conviction and confidence, being genuine and real, and staying true to yourself. As research professor Brené Brown says, "Authenticity is not something we have or don't have. It's a practice—a conscious choice of how we want to live. The choice to be honest, vulnerable, and let our true selves be seen."[63] In this chapter, we reveal the sixth key, *Be Your Authentic Self.* Here we explore why we disconnect from our true nature, what gets in our way of showing up authentic at work, and strategies for amplifying our authentic presence.

The False Self

Let's circle back to the formation of the human psyche noted in the previous chapter. We are born into this world in a state of pure awareness, innocence, and joy, connected to our true nature. We have an insatiable curiosity about our bodies, people, and surroundings, seeing the world with a beginner's mind. We can easily witness these essence qualities in a newborn baby. Babies exhibit this wonderment by playing with their feet, toys, and anything that engages their sensory perceptions. At an early age, we begin developing a set of beliefs of what is right and wrong, good and bad, appropriate and inappropriate, pleasant or unpleasant based on our experiences and messages we receive from our parents, siblings, or other people. We decide who we are and who we are not—creating what psychologists call ego boundaries. These boundaries help us stay safe from perceived danger, distinguish us from others, and prepare us for adulthood.

But, they also shield us from our true nature and essence qualities. This early conditioning influences our personality structure, which is made of patterns of thoughts, feelings, and behaviors that make us unique. These patterns become our default programming engrained in our brain chemistry, dictating how we show up in the world.

For example, if we've received messages from authority figures or influential people that we are smart, beautiful, strong, talented, important, and can achieve anything we want to, we will most likely have a healthy self-image, high self-esteem, and be successful in our careers and lives. However, if we've received messages that we are stupid, ugly, weak, untalented, unimportant, and we will never succeed in the world, we may struggle with an unhealthy self-image or low self-esteem. This leads us to doubt our instincts and lack confidence in our talents and abilities. Unfortunately, when our psychological needs of love, connection, autonomy, and belonging are not mirrored, nurtured or appreciated in our earlier years, we come to the conclusion something is wrong with us and we need to be fixed.

To compensate, we create a false self-image to adapt to our environment, get our needs met, and satisfy others' expectations. We may create an overinflated self-image of being better than others or a self-critical image that punishes us when we make a mistake. For instance, when you got straight As in school, your parents were happy and praised you with compliments or rewards. But, when you got Bs and Cs, your parents may have been disappointed and firmly lectured you about sabotaging your opportunity to get into a top university and be offered a high-paying job. This experience may precipitate your critical self-talk when you are not recognized as an "exceptional performer" in your job or do not receive the promotion you were promised.

We formulate these mental constructs of who we are and need to be at such a young age without understanding those impressions are the judgments and expectations of others and not sourced from our authentic nature. We begin projecting our fears and insecurities onto others from these past constructs: "You are lazy. You should work harder." Even worse, we begin judging ourselves harshly: "I am not smart enough" or "I am a failure." We deny or disown parts of ourselves that were not accepted or appreciated by others. We unconsciously take on this false self-image through school and our careers. After experiencing a life-altering event, such as an illness or death of a loved one, we may discover that we've lost touch with who we truly are, with our needs, and with what makes us happy. We may realize we have been living out the expectations of our parents to be successful in a particular field, such as medicine or business, only to discover those careers drain our energy and make us miserable. The ego boundaries and defenses we've created to protect our hearts and please others no longer support our needs for fulfillment. For instance, early in my career, I was driven by financial success with the hope to retire early and travel the world. It didn't matter if I loved my job. What mattered was a high-paying salary. This limited mindset only caused unrelenting stress and illness at the peak of my career. My drive for success overrode my heart desires for happiness and well-being.

During the global pandemic shelter-in-place, my clients had similar self-discoveries. Many found aspects of their life they neglected, such as exercise, sleep, healthy eating, hobbies, and raising a family due to the busyness of life. They realized they sacrificed cultivating their hearts' desires for the achievement of financial and career success. Research shows that living from a place of inauthenticity has its costs. When we create an insecure sense of self that continues to adapt to others' expectations, we develop a level of emotional exhaustion and distress from our constant emotional reactivity to negative events.[64] Our negativity bias creates hypervigilance to ensure we do the right thing and don't mess up or do something wrong in the future. Ultimately, we design a prison in our own minds that limits and restricts us from fully accessing our authentic power and the inner strengths of gratitude, kindness, compassion, sympathetic joy, and equanimity.

Our self-image also gets influenced and reinforced through our company performance systems and cultural norms. According to Marcus Buckingham's research on employee engagement, the mechanisms that companies use to measure performance, such as 360 assessments across core skill competencies, are not an effective measurement because these ratings generate bad data. They create what is called an "idiosyncratic rater effect," which means human beings are unreliable raters of other human beings. His research shows that when one person rates another person, over 60 percent of their rating is about them and not the person they're rating.

This becomes a big problem, especially when talent decisions, such as promotions, training, and deployment, are based on people's performance ratings, which are not an accurate reflection of their strengths and capabilities. These performance reviews, if not delivered in a way that honors our authenticity and full spectrum of capabilities—strengths, weaknesses, and growth areas—can further perpetuate feelings of unworthiness, imposter syndrome, and self-doubt. For example, many leaders I work with have received negative feedback from others who misrepresented or did not have full visibility of their achievements, only witnessing them in a handful of meetings. Sadly, this feedback did not provide a balanced view of their strengths and weaknesses and cost them a promotion. Instead, it made them question their expertise and capabilities rather than motivate them to grow their skills to elevate to the next leadership level.

Adapting to a new work culture brings up a host of inner struggles. We may have transitioned to a new team, got a new manager, or joined a new company only to find work gets done differently than how we learned in our previous jobs. This creates uncertainty and fear that we will make mistakes, not fit in, or not be recognized as a capable and talented contributor. The same strategies to be successful may be roadblocks in this new team or company. What got you to the place you are today will not get you where you want to go.

We must be adaptable and resilient without losing our authentic nature. However, sometimes too much adaptation can create dissonance with our true nature. In turn, we lose ourselves trying to fit into a culture that's not the best fit in the first place. For example, I was working as a senior manager for a team that required in-depth financial analysis, strategic framework, and solid recommendations backed by data insights for new projects to get funded by senior leadership. When I moved to another group, I was assigned to a large-scale initiative, and they valued an agile approach for testing new programs rather than providing long-term strategic planning and business-model design. The way they worked was dramatically different. Although I was still with the same company, it felt like I was in a new country learning a new language, set of rules, and how to navigate the city to avoid breaking any laws. The only way I was able to integrate into the new team was to let go of my past work patterns and learn the new group's work rules without compromising my values.

The Authentic Self

Eventually, most of us experience a breaking point in our career journey, which I refer to as a wake-up call. This wake-up call can show up as constant anxiety, overwhelm, illness, or burnout from being in a job that is not a good fit, is too demanding, not challenging, or not providing opportunities to add value. We can no longer endure this dissonance or incongruence with our authentic nature. This wake-up call will challenge and dismantle our false self-image, forcing us to honestly reexamine our choices, careers, lives, and relationships. As we engage in practices to discover our True North, recharge and nourish our bodies, calm the monkey mind, build emotional resilience, and cultivate a courageous heart, we begin remembering who we truly are. We meet the person we have been seeking all our lives—our authentic self. We let go of these false ideas of who we think we are. We stop adapting ourselves to meet other's expectations. We find we don't have to be right or win every debate or maintain power or social status. We start embracing our vulnerability, imperfections and perfections, and the innate strengths and capabilities of our authentic self. We grow the courage to meet our pain, failures, disappointments, or resentments with compassion, acceptance, and gratitude. We understand that challenges are a gift in disguise—a perfect formula for us to individuate as an adult and awaken to our destiny. This is the key to unlocking our authentic power and living our heart's desire. Like the hero in the hero's journey, it's the trials and tribulations that awaken us and help us evolve to become our best selves and make our unique mark in the world. It's like the caterpillar shedding its outer skin and moving into a cocoon or chrysalis to emerge into a beautiful butterfly. This metamorphosis is the miraculous process of adult development.

A great example of this transformation is portrayed in the American drama *Wonder*, the inspiring and heartwarming story of August "Auggie" Pullman, a ten-year-old boy living in Brooklyn, New York, who has a rare facial deformity. Throughout his young life, he undergoes twenty-seven different surgeries to allow him to see, smell, speak, and hear without a hearing aid. Home-schooled by his mother to nurture his early development, Auggie starts his fifth grade in a private school to integrate more with the world and socialize with other students.

At school, Auggie is bullied and ostracized by the other students, who call him a freak because of his physical appearance. Auggie continues to attend school despite the adversity. Eventually he builds strong friendships with two other kids. His sister encourages him to persevere: "You can't blend in when you were born to stand out." A pivotal moment comes during a three-day school adventure trip to a nature reserve. While the kids are watching a movie, Auggie and his friend sneak out to explore the forest. They are confronted by several seventh graders who mock Auggie, then attack him and his friend. Fearlessly, Auggie, who is only about four feet tall, stands up for himself and is willing to fight the seventh graders. Ironically, this courageous act is witnessed by the same students who have previously bullied him for his facial deformity. In this moment, they come to deeply respect Auggie for his courage and protect him from the older students. At the school graduation ceremony, Auggie is awarded the Henry Ward Beecher Medal for his demonstration of excellence and character in his schoolwork and relationships. He receives a standing ovation from his fellow students, faculty, and everyone in the audience.

You may resonate with Auggie's story, recalling a time when you were excluded at school or felt like an outsider at work. Perhaps you struggle fitting in at work because you feel threatened by your peers' education, experience, or strong personalities—questioning your own confidence. Or, you may not speak up or challenge a point of view in fear you will be shut down, fired, or excluded from the tribe. During the pandemic, you may have let go of old patterns that held you back and made new choices more aligned with your true nature. This is the wake-up call. As Auggie demonstrated, when we accept our authentic self, with all our imperfections and perfections, we can let go of hiding ourselves from others in fear of embarrassment and show up more powerfully and genuinely. When we are truly authentic, we demonstrate integrity, confidence, and courage with ourselves and others. It's our resistance and unwillingness to accept who we are that blocks us from deeper levels of fulfillment.

People will naturally gravitate to your imperfect character rather than the false masks or personas you may wear to fit in and belong to a group and culture. We need to belong to ourselves first without rejecting those qualities suppressed to survive as a child or not adequately nurtured by parents, teachers, society, and bosses. We forgive our caretakers or former bosses, understanding they did the best they could during that time. It's our human imperfections and vulnerabilities that connect us. We were born not to blend in but to standout in our full authentic power. This is the path of self-cultivation and self-actualization of our character and living our greatest potential unapologetically.

You may be thinking, "How do I bring my authentic self to work? or "How can I share my unique talents without holding back?" Here is a starting place. Experiment with these eight strategies to cultivate more authenticity, integrity, and courage as a leader and human being. It may feel challenging and uncomfortable at first. With consistent practice, you will feel more at ease and confident being authentically you at work and in life.

Cultivating Authenticity and Courage

1. **Align with your True North.** When we understand what makes us come alive, what gives us energy and passion, and why we are here on this planet, we align to our internal compass or drumbeat of our authentic being. We make choices from a place of integrity and discernment in times of uncertainty and challenge. Return to Key #1 to clarify your strengths, values, purpose, and vision. This will be your compass for navigating your life.

2. **Take personal responsibility.** It's easy to blame others for situations that go wrong. Being authentic means be-

ing open-minded, taking responsibility, extending an apology to mend a relationship, and learning from our mistakes. We refrain from attacking or judging someone who may disagree with our ideas. Embracing a "fail fast, learn faster" mindset, as learned from Jack Ma's success story, allows us to take accountability for our part in the situation and learn the lessons we want to apply in the future.

3. **Be courageously vulnerable.** Brené Brown says, "Vulnerability is the birthplace of love, belonging, joy, courage, empathy, and creativity. It is the source of hope, empathy, accountability, and authenticity. If we want greater clarity in our purpose and more meaningful lives, vulnerability is the path."[65] To be vulnerable is to be emotionally aware and to find the courage to express your true needs and feelings with others. If you disagree with a coworker about the direction of a project, you can demonstrate vulnerability by sharing your feelings and observations, why you disagree, and the impact it had on you, without judgment. It's not about venting your emotions or withholding your feelings to please another person. It's about being real, honest, and discerning, and taking a powerful stand for your experience.

4. **Trust your inner voice and body signals.** Our inner wisdom is always communicating to us. When we become more self-aware and aligned with our core values, our bodies will let us know if we are making the right decision or not. When I interviewed for jobs, I would evaluate whether the job was a good match for my skills, energy, and experience. I also reflected on whether the

company's culture and the hiring manager aligned to my core values and needs. If my body became unsettled, nauseated, or collapsed after an interview, I knew I needed to decline the offer because, in the long-term, I would be miserable. Earlier in my career, I was not attuned to my inner voice and would end up being stressed, burned out, and leaving the job feeling dissatisfied. A great question to ask when navigating the perfect role: "Does this job expand and strengthen me to be my authentic self, or does it drain and weaken me?" If the latter, I suggest you find another role or negotiate the role to play to your strengths.

5. **Be respectful and present.** As the old adage says, "Do unto others as you would have them do unto you." Treating people with respect is essential when building strong teams and relationships. You want to surround yourself with people who have your back through both good and tough times. If you aren't surrounded by those who are looking out for you, it's a good idea to have a courageous conversation with your team or manager or consider another team you can trust to support you during challenging situations. Showing respect is also about being present in your conversations. This means putting your devices away, bringing your full attention to the conversation, and truly connecting with the other person.

6. **Be confident in your own skin.** Not everyone is going to like you. Some may oppose your ideas and have strong opinions about you. Being authentic is not about being the most popular and likeable person. It's about

acting in integrity, being willing to make an unpopular decision or take an unpopular position, and speaking up with clarity, conviction, and compassion.

7. **Add value without bragging.** When you are less driven by the ego mind, you have little tolerance for people who lie, play office politics, or brag about their accomplishments. Gaining visibility in large companies often requires showcasing our accomplishments in a public forum, which can be uncomfortable, especially since society has conditioned us to view tooting our own horn in a negative light. If you need to increase your visibility with senior leaders, demonstrate your value by focusing on what your team did to add value to customers and the business rather than taking the credit. Let your merits speak for themselves. Your true value will be apparent without you having to point it out.

8. **Amplify your authentic brand.** Once you understand who you are and are aligned to your authentic presence, you can create your personal brand and share it with your peers, potential employers, and social circles. Combining your strengths, values, purpose, and skills makes for a compelling brand statement you can use in meetings, conferences, interviews, and on social media. It's important to showcase your strengths along with the value or impact you deliver to your target audience. For example, if you are an engineer, your brand may be "I build innovative and sustainable technology solutions that grow customers' businesses while preserving the environment." If you are a sales leader, your brand may be "I build high-performing teams that exceed customer

expectations while generating unprecedented growth." In some cases, your brand and purpose statement may be the same. Test out your brand with your peers. See how it lands and get feedback on the strengths and value you bring to your team and company. You will know you landed on the right brand when you feel a deep resonance and aliveness in your body. Our personal brand is not static, it changes as we grow and evolve in our careers.

Ultimately, as we align to our authentic self, we exude more confidence, optimism, gratitude, and humility. We have more capacity to adapt to situations and see the silver linings. We are more courageous and willing to learn about our thoughts, feelings, and needs and build more mastery in our talents. We become more generous in sharing resources and helping others grow, succeed, and contribute in meaningful ways that amplify their uniqueness and strengths. When we stand out, we liberate others to do the same. We pay it forward. This, my friend, is the key to ending the cycle of burnout—being authentically you. Now you are ready to play your bigger game and translate the wisdom and insights you've gleaned from the previous chapters into an actionable roadmap to achieve greater success and happiness.

Reflections

- What does it mean to be authentically you? What are those qualities or behaviors?
- What stops you from showing those qualities or behaviors at work or in life?
- What self-image do you need to let go of to embrace your authentic self?
- What strategies can help you cultivate more authenticity, integrity, and courage?
- Define your authentic brand statement. Include your strengths, the audience you serve, and the impact or value you deliver. For example:
  - "I build innovative solutions that solve customer challenges while creating double-digit growth."
  - "I transform how we work, live, and play through artificial-intelligence technologies."
  - "I build dynamic learning solutions to help people grow their potential and contribute to the world in meaningful ways."
  - "I build sustainable technology solutions that reduce our carbon footprint and provide a healthy planet for future generations."
- Promote your brand. Add it to your résumés and social media platforms or while networking at social events or business meetings.

KEY #7

Create Your Roadmap to Success and Happiness

*If you want to be truly happy, set compelling goals that liberate
your authentic self and inspire you to wake up every morning
grateful to be alive.*

Now that you have gathered six of the seven keys for unlocking your greatest potential, we are going to put everything into action by creating a roadmap to achieve your life vision. Creating goals is probably not new to you, especially in business. However, it may be new when it comes to achieving your life aspirations. Without a clear, tangible roadmap to pave your path to success and happiness, your vision is only a wish. As Steven Covey says, "As you climb the ladder of success be sure it's leaning against the right building."[66] In this chapter, I uncover the seventh and final key, *Create Your Roadmap to Success and Happiness*. This will guide you in living your destiny. We will explore why common rituals such as setting resolutions don't work. And how a science-based goal-setting approach is a better alternative for producing positive habits and behavioral changes that are aligned with our purpose and vision.

Most of us have probably tried the ritual of New Year's resolutions, where we state our intentions for the coming year, such as losing weight, saving money, buying a home, starting a family, or traveling to a new bucket-list location only to be disappointed after thirty days. According to a recent U.S. News & World Report article, New Year's resolutions fail about 80 percent of the time, with most people having lost their resolve by mid-February.[67]

Why are resolutions destined to fail? First, the changes we want to make require changing behaviors that are deeply rooted in the neurological circuitry in our brains. We often heard it takes twenty-one days to change a habit or behavior, but health psychologist Philippa Lally's research suggests otherwise. He discovered that although some habits can change within twenty-one days, it generally takes longer to rewire neural connections—in some cases up to eight months.[68]

Another challenge is that the behaviors we want to change (such as overindulging in food, sugar, and alcohol, spending money beyond our means, working too many hours, or excessively using social media) self-soothe us in some way. They activate our brain's neurotransmitter dopamine as previously noted. Unfortunately, our short-term gratification from these experiences only creates a false sense of happiness, perpetuating unhealthy habits. Giving up these addictive patterns can be challenging and can trigger subconscious feelings and thoughts of self-doubt, anxiety, or depression, which often block us from achieving our goals.

Resolutions can also be ineffective when too vague or unrealistic or when we don't have others supporting our new positive changes, which may foster discouragement, fear of failure, and isolation. Hence, we give up early, make excuses, let go of our desires, and regress to old habits and comfort zones to satisfy our needs. Sadly, New Year's resolutions don't lead to sustainable behavior change, nor do they harness the motivation that inspires action.

A mindful alternative to realize your vision is creating meaningful goals that are specific, actionable, and purposeful. To get started, try these seven steps for creating your roadmap to success and happiness to ensure lasting behavior change and long-term fulfillment.

1. **Harvest past-year successes and learnings.** Before creating your goals, write down all of your successes and learnings from the past year. Identify any behaviors or disappointments you want to let go of, as well as any behaviors you want to start and continue in the new year. It's best to start the new year with a fresh perspective and clean slate, with no regrets.

2. **Clarify your life vision.** Clarify what you want to experience in the new year. In Key #1, you created your life vision, purpose, and the areas you want to change using the Life Compass Map. This assessment focused on your physical, emotional, mental, and spiritual health and well-being, and on your career, service, primary relationship, other relationships, finances, and leisure. Based on your assessment, identify what areas in your life need more attention for you to experience more happiness and fulfillment.

3. **Create clear goals and actions.** Once you understand where you are today and where you want to be in the future, it's time to clarify the specific goals and actions you need to take to get to your desired outcome. An effective method for creating goals is making them SMART (specific, measurable, achievable, realistic, and timely). I often suggest focusing on three to five goals, depending on your capacity to follow through on your commitments. Making your goals realistic and achievable sets you up for success. If you have a large goal, such as a home remodel, think about breaking it down into specific

categories or actions, like a project plan, to help you more easily achieve that goal. Leverage any of the practices and strategies from the previous chapters to spark ideas. It's important for the goals to be stated positively and in the present tense because the brain cannot decipher the difference between negative and positive. For example, instead of saying, "I will stop eating junk food," try "I will eat healthy foods that support optimal health." It's also important to hold your goals lightly. This allows flexibility for you to pivot if unexpected circumstances, such as a global pandemic, arise. Goals are signposts to move you forward, not roadblocks to keep you stuck. Examples include:

- Health: Improve my health, stress levels, and well-being within healthy biomarker ranges by (date).
  - Work forty hours per week, reserving time for family, fun, rest, and exercise.
  - Eat a healthy, organic diet aligned to my personalized health plan.
- Career: Get promoted to director of customer experience to increase my leadership impact and establish more financial success by (date).
  - Align director-level job expectations with my manager.
  - Expand business knowledge in software subscription models.
- Service: Start a nonprofit organization to support underserved communities by (date).
  - Develop a business plan to secure funding.

- Select five board members who will support fundraisers.
- Finances: Buy a beautiful home in the suburbs to raise a family by (date).
    - Save $50,000 to have sufficient funds for a down payment.
    - Get a real-estate agent to find a home that meets my criteria.
- Relationships: Be more effective in managing challenging relationships and creating win-win outcomes by (date).
    - Apply the practices on emotional intelligence or take a communications course.
    - Practice delivering constructive feedback to at least four people.

4. **Define your powerful why.** Define why each goal is important to inspire motivation and momentum. For instance: Being a director in my organization enables me to make a difference in people's lives, grow my unique strengths, and support my children's education. Or: purchasing a home in the suburbs will allow us to start a family, be close to hiking trails and schools, and be part of a community of like-minded people.

5. **Take action.** To reinforce new behaviors and habits, incorporate your actions into your calendar. Goals are useless if they stay in your notebook without applying to your everyday life. Without consistent action, you will most likely be discouraged and slip into old habits.

6. **Get an accountability partner.** Having someone in your corner, such as a coach or mentor, who believes in your

brilliance and holds you accountable will accelerate your progress and help you overcome roadblocks and limiting mindsets. This is especially important when old habits or your inner critic sneak in to sabotage your efforts.

7. **Celebrate your successes.** Every time you make progress toward your goals, find a way to celebrate your success. Treat yourself to a delicious dinner, massage, concert, or weekend getaway to celebrate all the hard work you invested in making these positive changes. This will stimulate dopamine, build resilience, and keep you on track for achieving your goals.

For our goals and actions to create lasting change, we need to ensure we create lasting, positive habits. As author of *Atomic Habits*, James Clear, says, "Your life is essentially the sum of your habits. How happy or unhappy, successful or unsuccessful, or healthy and unhealthy you are, is the result of your habits."[69] Neuroscience research supports the effectiveness of the following four-step approach for creating positive habits: cue, craving, response, and reward.

The first step is to identify a cue or trigger that helps you remember to do the new habit and understand the benefit you will gain from doing it. For example, you want to start a meditation practice but find it extremely challenging due to your busy schedule. It will be difficult to keep up the practice. However, if you associate a desired outcome with doing the meditation practice, like more relaxation, creativity, presence, and productivity at work, you will be more committed to following through. Establishing helpful cues or reminders, such as practice every morning or at lunchtime, will reinforce the new habit. With consistent practice, you will be more motivated to practice meditation because of the positive results: increased mental clarity and deep relaxation or comments from others on how clear and influential you are in meetings.

This precipitates a craving, which is step two in creating habits. Now that your brain has experienced pleasure or satisfaction, you will be motivated to do it again. The brain loves repetition. For instance, I use to resist hiking alone in the redwoods or along the coast until I teamed up with a friend and started feeling invigorated, grounded, healthier, and happier; it became easy and appealing for me to commit to that action one or two times a week. Our cues trigger cravings that ultimately motivate us to respond or take action to receive a reward that satisfies our craving. This repetition of an activity produces new neural connections, overwriting the old, unproductive or negative habits over time. This is neuroplasticity in action.

It's also important to create actions or habits that are obvious, attractive, easy, and satisfying. For each action, I suggest you establish satisfying rewards to cultivate momentum and excitement and avoid resorting to old behaviors that do not promote long-term fulfillment. If you are not excited about or not enjoying doing your actions, it will be difficult to motivate you to stay the course to obtain your goals, causing you to make excuses, procrastinate, or give up altogether. For example, you may want to start a yoga practice to improve your health and energy levels. You will be more successful if you select a style of yoga you enjoy, such as vinyasa, ashtanga, or yin yoga and commit to a routine, such as every Monday, Wednesday, and Friday. You can reward yourself with a delicious meal at your favorite restaurant after every thirty days. Our brains also love routines. Establishing structures will help you create new, positive habits at a cellular level and accelerate the attainment of your desired outcomes.

With your roadmap to success and happiness established, let's now explore how to navigate potential roadblocks with resilience and discernment to achieve your goals and live your destined path.

Reflections

- What are three to five goals you want to achieve in the next year that will help you realize your vision? What is your powerful why behind achieving these goals?

- What actions are you committed to doing for each goal? Be sure to leverage any of the mindful strategies, tools, and practices from previous chapters.

- What old habits do you need to let go of to achieve your goals? What new habits do you need to embrace to create positive, lasting change?

- Who will be your accountability partner that helps ensure you stay on track?

- What routines or structures can you create to make your new habits stick over time?

- How will you reward yourself when you achieve your goals and actions?

OBSTACLES
Navigating Your Path

When we step outside our comfort zone, we can experience a
whole new level of freedom, joy, and aliveness.

In 2010, I was leading the biggest global business-transformation initiative of my career. It was aimed at transforming the customer-order-
ing-management process from a semimanual system using spreadsheets
and web-applications to full business-to-business automation. With
an approximately $200 million annual roadmap and major changes to
cross-functional teams, systems, and processes, I led the change management scope of work and was chartered to establish a single change-man-
agement-operating-model to roll out the new ordering capabilities to
our internal and external customers. This change was unprecedented in
the company's history. Overwhelmed, stressed, and way out of my comfort zone, I sought guidance from a top change-consulting firm to help
navigate this transformation. Asking for help was the best decision I
made. It saved me from burning out again, avoiding future health challenges, and risking my reputation. In the past, I would have endured
the overwhelm, ignored my body signals and inner voice, and tried to
do it alone. Applying the seven keys, I was smarter, wiser, and no longer
interested in being the lone hero who drove business results at a huge
emotional cost.

In this chapter, we will explore the potential roadblocks you may encounter as you implement your roadmap to living your destiny. I hope your roadmap makes you feel energized and inspired to wake up each morning and live your purpose with passion and courage.

Anytime we commit to making positive changes in our life, our brain becomes super engaged, evaluating any potential danger or risks in your decisions or external environment. This essential survival mechanism is hardwired in our brain neurology to keep us safe. However, it can also be a roadblock to achieving our dreams. Our old stories of fear of failure, not being good enough, imposter syndrome, rejection, and self-doubt will naturally come up. Feelings of stress, anxiety, and even overwhelm can show up as we step out of our comfort zones. Remember, our brain's limbic region, the emotional brain, keeps a database of memories from early childhood. Our fear of reliving those experiences will be more exaggerated, prompting our limbic brain to sabotage our new, positive habits and behaviors. For instance, you may want to start up a nonprofit organization with underserved communities, and your self-talk, says, "Who are you to start up a nonprofit organization?" or "It's a waste of time. You will fail anyways." These subconscious messages may sound familiar, as if you are hearing them from a critical parent or unsupportive boss. Know that these self-talk messages are common and you are not losing your mind. Whenever we embark on anything new, especially something that may radically shift our way of being or thinking, resistance will arise and try to stop us from moving forward. This may come in the form of procrastinating, forgetting or deprioritizing our actions or practices, making excuses, binge-watching Netflix, or simply giving up. In other words, we regress into our comfort zones.

Our comfort zone is a psychological state where we feel familiar, in control of our environment, and experience low levels of anxiety and stress. It's our safe place to return to when we are exhausted and afraid that something bad or dangerous will happen. Although this place feels safe, it's also the area where we can feel too complacent, unchallenged, lifeless, or afraid of risk-taking. We end up doing the same thing over and over again with minimal growth in our life or work performance. The dream of getting to the next leadership level, writing a book that makes a difference, traveling to new countries, or starting a nonprofit gets shelved on the "someday" list. This can also lead us to compare ourselves to others, feeling envious, and wishing we were experiencing similar success, happiness, and aliveness.

Your roadmap is intended to get you out of your comfort zone and into your growth zone. This is where the new activities or habits you start doing may feel awkward and unfamiliar yet provide a level of challenge and excitement for learning to occur. It will expand your skills, mindset, and boundaries and allow you to reach a whole new level of potential. This zone is a space for opportunity and personal transformation. Operating in your growth zone allows you to take on new and bigger job assignments, get married and have children, start that nonprofit with help from a mentor, go back to school and get your master's degree, or take on new lifestyle practices, such as meditation, yoga, exercise, and eating healthy. In this zone, you will usually feel exhilarated and alive, but also uncertain and nervous because you do not have a reference point from a past experience. A growth mindset is required to overcome fear of failure, self-doubt, and any negative thinking. Over time, we develop the courage, confidence, and capability to walk through our fears and make our dreams a reality.

In some cases, we set overly ambitious goals that are way out of our comfort zone and we end up in our panic zone. An example might be taking on a leadership role with a larger scope, such as leading a team of thirty globally when you only led a team of five in one geographic region. By overstretching our boundaries and abilities, we can experience extreme overwhelm and possibly traumatic memories from the past and not have the capacity to manage difficult situations. This activates the fight-flight-or-freeze stress response, creating feelings of frustration, anxiety, anger, aggression, and exhaustion; physical sensations such as rapid heart rate and scattered thinking; and even shutting down. When the overwhelm is too intense, learning and growth become nearly impossible. As psychologist Robert Yerkes says, "Anxiety improves performance until a certain optimum level of arousal has been reached. Beyond that point, performance deteriorates as higher levels of anxiety are attained."[70]

As we traverse our career journey, we want to find our growth zone to gradually grow into the next level of mastery. We do not want to leap too far outside our growth zone to where we become paralyzed by stress and anxiety. This is the birthplace of burnout. Of course, these psychological zones depend on an individual's past experiences, capabilities, and their capacity to endure change and stress. I have a friend who will travel to third-world countries by herself with ease and joy, while I would panic and think about all the things that could go wrong, such as getting food poisoning or being held hostage. However, when I traveled with a group of people to Bali on a yoga retreat, my fear subsided and I felt safe and energized. The trip ended up being a life-changing experience, and I was truly grateful I had the courage to move through my fears. When we step outside our comfort zones, we can experience a whole new level of freedom, joy, and aliveness.

Although change happens outside our comfort zone, it does not have to be hard. It can be fun and exhilarating, like an adventure to a new country. Applying the seven keys outlined in this book will help you end the cycle of burnout; anchor to your True North (your purpose, strengths, values, vision); build the physical, mental, emotional, and intuitive capacities to continuously evolve into your most authentic and greatest self; and live a meaningful career and life. Creating positive habits by establishing cues, actions, routines, and rewards will help you shift your negative mindsets or unproductive habits to new positive mindsets and productive habits that promote lasting fulfillment. What makes this challenging is that we often cannot see our blind spots or unconscious thinking or emotional patterns, and it's easy to fall into old habitual patterns.

As I learned in my corporate career, asking for help takes tremendous courage. It accelerates our growth and performance in ways that support our aspirations and well-being. Qualified leadership coaches will fast-track your results by championing you, holding you accountable, and challenging you to step out of your comfort zone to grow to the next level of mastery. They are an unbiased sounding board to help you explore your ideas and challenges in a safe and confidential space. They can help you see your strengths and blind spots more clearly and partner with you on building new mindsets and skills for dealing with challenges and preparing you for the next level. Whether you are an individual contributor moving to a team-leader role or a director moving to a vice-president role, having someone by your side will elevate you and expedite your learning and integration process. What got you where you are today will most likely not get you where you want to be. That's where a seasoned coach can help break through blind spots, excuses, or perceived limitations.

Another great strategy in navigating your career is building a group of supporters to champion your success. These supporters include a sponsor, internal mentor, and peer network. A sponsor is a senior leader who will advocate for you during talent reviews or succession planning meetings. This person can endorse your skills, capabilities, character, and contributions with their leadership team: "Samantha is a solid candidate for that director role. She has a stellar track record in managing complex customer accounts and growing the business. I personally witnessed her manage tough customer issues with diplomacy and courage." Having a sponsor helps open doors faster than advocating solely by yourself.

On the other hand, an internal mentor can help you navigate the company culture and share the lessons they learned for rising to the next level. Many senior leaders enjoy giving back and helping high-potential leaders or individual contributors accelerate their career progression. To select the right mentor, consider a leader who has the job skills, expertise and experience you want to grow into in the next two years, shares similar values, and knows how to maneuver corporate politics. Lastly, build a network of peers across business functions. Schedule periodic meetings to provide support on work challenges or projects, share best practices, and champion each other's success. Working together to learn, grow and traverse your careers is more exciting than doing it alone.

When navigating your career path, know you can leverage any of the seven keys anytime. You can pivot your roadmap to remain relevant in the workplace and marketplace, build your team of supporters, and go back to your comfort zone to recharge and reset. Life is not a destination it is a journey. Remember, you can manage the pace of your career without burning out and be the master of your career destiny. Let's now explore how to live a life with no regrets.

CONCLUSION
Live a Life
without Regret

*Choose a life that liberates your dreams, makes you come alive,
and allows you to feel the depths of the joy, love, and vulnerability
of being human.*

Bronnie Ware, author of *The Top Five Regrets of the Dying*, shares her observations as an Australian nurse providing palliative care to patients in the last twelve weeks of their life. The number-one regret, these patients confessed, was not having the courage to live a life true to themselves and living the life others expected of them. Most people did not honor even half of their dreams due to the choices they made. The second regret was working hard and spending most of their lives pursuing their career ambitions and not tending to what mattered most. The third regret was not having the courage to express their feelings in their relationships and allowing bitterness and resentment to fester in their hearts. The fourth regret was not having invested the time or effort in sustaining strong, meaningful friendships, and finding themselves alone in the last weeks of their lives. The final regret: they wished they allowed themselves to be happier. The fear of change kept them safe and complacent when deep inside they longed to laugh, be silly, and feel the thrill of being alive.[71]

The seven keys are guideposts for creating not only successful and mindful careers with resilience but also finding genuine happiness and cultivating greater health and well-being. They build a solid foundation for cultivating the strengths, skills, and physical, mental, emotional and intuitive capacities needed to play your best game at work and in life.

The first key, *Find Your True North*, is foundational. Crystalizing your life purpose, unique strengths, core values, and life vision ignites the energy and passion you will need to overcome obstacles on your path. It anchors you in our inherent joy and aliveness, as well as serves as your inner compass to traverse your career. Aligning with your True North will enable you to grow your talents to new heights, find meaning in your work, and make the difference you dreamed of making in this world. It is your "powerful why" for living your best life every day. Your True North will be your source of inspiration to persevere, even on your toughest days when you want to give up.

The second key, *Put Your Oxygen Mask On First*, is essential to be engaged, creative, and effective at work without burning out. Applying self-care and time-management strategies, such as prioritizing your workload, saying no, blocking focus time, letting go of stressors, and filling your joy cup, will help you manage the unpredictable demands of work and life with more resilience. Having clear boundaries and work-life balance will sustain your energy levels while supporting your personal needs as well as the needs of your family, boss, and colleagues.

The third key, *Recharge and Nourish Your Body*, is the gateway to revitalizing your energy, replenishing your well-being, and accessing your body intelligence. We investigated how the brain works, what happens during a stressful event, and mind-body strategies to end the cycle of burnout. We explored the benefits of restorative sleep and how to reset your circadian rhythms and be resilient to tackle your busy schedule. We uncovered mind-body practices, such as yoga and qigong, for creating more flexibility, strength, relaxation, and well-being. These practices deepen your mind-body awareness and intuitive capacities to hear your authentic voice more clearly. We wrapped up this chapter by showing you how cardio exercise, especially in nature, and an organic whole-food diet help you stay healthy, strong, and perform at your best.

The fourth key, *Master the Monkey Mind,* is the cornerstone for unlocking your greatest potential. We examined how to shift negative mindsets that lead to stress, burnout, and undesirable outcomes to positive mindsets that leads to balance, happiness and desirable outcomes. We explored how fears of self-doubt, failure, and not being enough will naturally arise when you move outside your comfort zones and elevate to the next level. Cultivating a quiet mind and growth mindset will help you face your fears and inner critic with compassion and transform your resistance into courage and wisdom. The mindfulness strategies, such as meditation, taking energy breaks, harvesting the good experiences, and unplugging from digital devices will help you stay focused, calm, positive, and present in this fast-paced VUCA world.

The fifth key, *Grow a Resilient and Courageous Heart,* explores how to build emotional resilience by increasing self-awareness, regulating your emotional reactions, having courageous conversations, and building more trusting relationships. We uncovered the importance of cultivating the inner strengths of gratitude, loving-kindness, compassion, sympathetic joy, and equanimity to navigate stressful situations, setbacks, and uncertainty with a brave heart.

The sixth key, *Be Your Authentic Self,* reveals the importance of aligning to our authentic nature by bravely being ourselves at work. We explored the importance of anchoring to our True North; taking personal responsibility for our actions; being courageously vulnerable, respectful, and present in our relationships; and trusting our inner voice and body signals when navigating important decisions. When we ground in our true nature, we are more confident in sharing our unique strengths and talents with our teams, families, and the broader world. We can embrace our innate gifts and shortcomings, and celebrate the fullness of who we are. We begin speaking the hard truth and not withholding our voice in the midst of challenge or conflict. We begin listening to our intuitive guidance rather than our impulsive desires for short-term gratification. We rise above the unproductive politics and lead with empathy and integrity—doing what's right for the benefit of others. As we embody our authentic presence, we navigate our journey with more clarity and conviction— taking a stand for what matters most.

The seventh key, *Create Your Roadmap to Success and Happiness,* integrates the previous six keys into a practical plan to keep your dreams alive and attainable. We've explored a mindful approach for crafting clear goals, actions, and positive habits to realize your life vision. When we have a plan on what we want in life, we are more intentional with our choices and actions. Whatever we focus our attention on, naturally grows. We plant the seeds to harvest our dreams while staying grounded in the present moment. This roadmap is not set in stone, it changes as your life evolves. It allows you to pivot and navigate potential obstacles along your journey and stay in your growth zone to create sustainable, positive change. Surrounding yourself with supporters—a coach, mentors, or peers—is essential. They can celebrate, champion, and have your back, especially when you want to give up on your dreams and regress to old ways.

My sincere wish for you is to create a life that ignites your deepest heart desire—inspired by a meaningful purpose in this changing world. May you have the courage and resilience to move through your fears and setbacks and live the life you were born to live with no regrets. May you look back at your life and find gratitude that you invested the energy and effort to live your unique purpose. May you explore your greatest potential and be resilient in starting over again and again, even after difficult failures. And have the humility to ask for help along the way. May you be courageous enough to be vulnerable, share your authentic feelings and surround yourself with people who truly have your back and will champion your dreams. May you create a life that makes you happy and allows you to feel the drumbeat of your soul and the ecstatic joy of being authentically you.

The world awaits your magnificence as you play your best game and make your unique contribution. Together, we will recreate a new future for our careers, lives, children, and world.

Acknowledgments

I was inspired to write this book to empower and educate people about the cycle of stress and burnout and provide an integrated roadmap of evidence-based, practical tools to help them live meaningful careers and lives with resilience and fulfillment. This book would not have been possible without my inner guidance and the many who inspired me, championed me, and shared their wisdom with me along my life journey.

A big thanks to all my amazing coaching clients who had the courage to step into their most authentic and powerful selves and play their bigger game to make a difference for themselves and their teams, businesses, families, and the world. I am inspired by your brilliance, authenticity, and tenacity to create wildly successful careers!

Thank you to three companies that had a huge influence and impact on my career. First, the Marcus Buckingham Company—thank you for the opportunity to coach leaders using a strengths-based approach and to be part of the talent revolution for redefining the future of work. Next, my deep gratitude to Potential Project for the opportunity to facilitate mindfulness workshops rooted in neuroscience and research to help people build emotional resilience and enhance their mental performance in this changing world. A huge thank you to Cisco and my former managers, for an incredible corporate career leading global transformation initiatives and now as an external executive coach to help leaders grow their strengths and skills to lead their teams and businesses with greater confidence.

A deep bow of gratitude to the wisdom teachers I studied with, specifically Jon Bernie, Roma Hammel, Hameed Almaas, Jack Kornfield, and Russ Hudson. Collectively, you taught me personal transformation and mindfulness strategies for cultivating awareness, generosity, authenticity, and compassion. A special thanks to Jennifer Prugh for being an inspirational teacher and friend who emulates living in alignment to a deeper purpose with compassion, generosity, and courage. You've inspired me to surrender to my purpose wholeheartedly.

I am incredibly grateful for Dr. Greg Hammer for writing the foreword in this book and his partnership in piloting a mindfulness program at Stanford University. Together we've helped physicians reduce job stress and burnout while building more resilience and effectiveness in delivering quality care to patients.

Much gratitude to those who supported this book project. The Eschler Editing team for their thoughtful editorial feedback, guidance, and getting my book ready for publishing. Jeanne-Marie for her friendship and brilliant feedback to ensure the book communicates the key messages clearly and powerfully. Kelly for being an incredible friend and sounding board for helping me shape the book concept and interior design. Chris for his friendship and being an early reader to ensure the book captured the essence of burnout and the path of awakening.

Finally, a big thank-you to my family, including my parents, Nancy, Linda, Jackie, and Lauren for their unconditional love and encouragement. I am grateful for my healthcare providers, especially Dr. Mindy Pelz, functional medicine chiropractor. Without her guidance and education on ancient and natural healing methods, I would have been stressed and burned out and not had the tools to transform my health and live my purpose with vitality and passion.

References

Bradberry, Travis and Greaves, Jean, *Emotional Intelligence 2.0* (San Diego: Talent Smart, 2009).

Clear, James, *Atomic Habits: An Easy & Proven Way to Build Good Habits & Break Bad Ones* (New York: Penguin Random House, 2018).

Fung, Dr. Jason, *Diabetes Code: Prevent and Reverse Type Diabetes Naturally* (British Columbia: Greystone Books Ltd., 2018).

Goleman, Daniel, *Emotional Intelligence: Why It Can Matter More Than IQ* (New York: Bantam Books, 1995).

Goodall, Ashley and Buckingham, Marcus, *Nine Lies about Work* (Boston: Harvard Business Review Press, 2019).

Hanson, Rick, *Hardwiring Happiness* (New York: Crown Publishing Group, 2013).

Hyman, Dr. Mark Hyman, *Food: What the Heck Should I Eat?* (New York: Hachette Book Group, 2018).

Siegel, Daniel, *Mindful Brain* (New York: Mind Your Brain, Inc., 2007).

Notes

1. Warren Bennis and Burt Nanus, *Leaders: Strategies for Taking Charge* (New York: HarperCollins Publishers, 2003).
2. Edward Hallowell, "Overloaded Circuits: Why Smart People Underperform", Harvard Business Review, January 2005.
3. Marija Kojic, "Career Burnout and Its Effect on Health," Clokify, June 7, 2019, https://clockify.me/blog/productivity/career-burnout/.
4. Ryan Pendell, "Millennials Are Burning Out," Workplace, July 19, 2018, https://www.gallup.com/workplace/237377/millennials-burning.aspx.
5. Mayo Clinic Staff, "Job Burnout: How to Spot It and Take Action," Mayo Clinic, November 21, 2018, https://www.mayoclinic.org/healthy-lifestyle/adult-health/in-depth/burnout/art-20046642.
6. Michael Blanding, "National Health Costs Could Decrease if Managers Reduce Work Stress," Harvard Business School, January 26, 2015, https://hbswk.hbs.edu/item/national-health-costs-could-decrease-if-managers-reduce-work-stress
7. Mayo Clinic Staff, "Job Burnout: How to Spot It and Take Action," Mayo Clinic, November 21, 2018, https://www.mayoclinic.org/healthy-lifestyle/adult-health/in-depth/burnout/art-20046642.

8. Mayo Clinic Staff, "Job Burnout: How to Spot It and Take Action," Mayo Clinic, November 21, 2018, https://www.mayoclinic.org/healthy-lifestyle/adult-health/in-depth/burnout/art-20046642.

9. Deepak Chopra, The Awakening, YouTube, November 10, 2014, https://www.youtube.com/watch?v=04jlC-8jxHQ.

10. Joseph Campbell, *The Hero with a Thousand Faces in The Collected Works of Joseph Campbell* (Novato: New World Library, 2008).

11. Isaacson, Walter, *Steve Jobs* (New York: Simon & Schuster Paperbacks, 2011).

12. Jim Harter, "4 Factors Driving Record-High Employee Engagement U.S.", Gallup Workplace, February 4, 2020, https://www.gallup.com/workplace/284180/factors-driving-record-high-employee-engagement.aspx.

13. Jim Harter, "4 Factors Driving Record-High Employee Engagement in U.S.," Gallup Workplace, February 4, 2020, https://www.gallup.com/workplace/284180/factors-driving-record-high-employee-engagement.aspx.

14. Ashley Goodall and Marcus Buckingham, *Nine Lies about Work* (Boston: Harvard Business Review Press, 2019).

15. Ibid.

16. Victor E. Frankl, *Man's Search for Meaning* (Boston: Beacon Press, 2006).

17. Mark Zuckerberg, "Bringing the World Closer Together," Mark Zuckerberg Blog, June 22, 2017, https://www.facebook.com/notes/mark-zuckerberg/bringing-the-world-closer-together/.

18. "Mental Contrasting: The Good, The Bad, and The Ugly," Happier Human, March 23, 2020, https://www.happierhuman.com/mental-contrasting/.

19. Tchiki Davis, "What Is Well-Being? Definition, Types, and Well-Being Skills," Psychology Today, January 2, 2019, https://www.psychologytoday.com/gb/blog/click-here-happiness/201901/what-is-well-being-definition-types-and-well-being-skills.

20. Joseph Juran, "Pareto Principle (80/20 Rule) & Pareto Analysis Guide," Juran, March 12, 2019, https://www.juran.com/blog/a-guide-to-the-pareto-principle-80-20-rule-pareto-analysis/.

21. Daniel Siegel, *Mindful Brain* (New York: Mind Your Brain, Inc., 2007).

22. Harvard Medical School, "Understanding the Stress Response," Harvard Health Publishing, July 6, 2020.

23. Daniel Goleman, *Emotional Intelligence: Why It Can Matter More Than IQ*, (New York: Bantam Books, 1995).

24. Peter A. Levine, *In an Unspoken Voice: How the Body Releases Trauma and Restores Goodness* (Berkeley: North Atlantic Books, 2020).

25. Karin Roelofs, "Freeze for Action: Neurobiological Mechanisms in Animal and Human Freezing", US National Library of Medicine, April 19, 2017, https://pubmed.ncbi.nlm.nih.gov/28242739/.

26. Aaron Lerner, Sandra Neidhofer, and Torsten Matthias, "The Gut Microbiome Feelings of the Brain: A Perspective for Non-Microbiologists," US National Library of Medicine, https://www.ncbi.nlm.nih.gov/pmc/articles/PMC5748575/

27. Institute of Medicine Committee on Sleep Medicine and Research, "Extent and Health Consequences of Chronic Sleep Loss and Sleep Disorders," US National Academy of Sciences, 2006, https://www.ncbi.nlm.nih.gov/books/NBK19961/.

28. Goran Medic, Micheline Wille, and Michiel Hemels, "Short- and Long-Term Health Consequences of Sleep Disruption," US National Library of Medicine, 2017, https://www.ncbi.nlm.nih.gov/pmc/articles/PMC5449130/.

29. Melinda Smith, Lawrence Robinson, and Robert Segal, HealthGuideOrg International, June 2019, https://www.helpguide.org/articles/sleep/sleep-needs-get-the-sleep-you-need.htm.

30. Julie Hand, "This Yoga Routine Will Make You Feel Like You Got A Full Night's Sleep," Bulletproof, March 20, 2018, https://www.bulletproof.com/sleep/sleep-hacks/yoga-nidra-guided-sleep-meditation/#ref-4

31. Apar Avinash Saoji, B. R. Raghavendra, and N.K. Manjunath, "Effects of Yogic Breath Regulation: A Narrative Review of Scientific Evidence," *Journal of Ayurveda and Integrative Medicine*, January–March 2019, https://www.sciencedirect.com/science/article/pii/S0975947617303224?via%3Dihub.

32. Seyed Giliani and Abdurrashid Feizabad, "The Effects of Aerobic Exercise Training on Mental Health and Self-Esteem of Type 2 Diabetes Mellitus Patients," US National Academy of Sciences, March 19, 2019, https,//www.ncbi.nlm.nih.gov/pmc/articles/PMC6441819/.

33. Richard Louv, *Last Child in the Woods: Saving Our Children from Nature-Deficit Disorder* (New York: Workman Publishing, 2008).

34. Gregory Bratman, J. Paul Hamilton, Kevin Hahn, Gretch Daily, and James Gross, "Nature Experience Reduces Rumination and Subgenual Prefrontal Cortex Activation," Proceedings of National Academy of Sciences of USA, July 14, 2015, https://www.pnas.org/content/112/28/8567.

35. Ryan Raman, "How to Safely Get Vitamin D from Sunlight," Healthline, April 28, 2018, https://www.healthline.com/nutrition/vitamin-d-from-sun.

36. Madhuleena Roy Chowdhury, "The Positive Effects of Nature On Your Mental Well-being," PositivePsychology, June 5, 2020, https://positivepsychology.com/positive-effects-of-nature/.

37. Dr. Mark Hyman, *Food: What the Heck Should I Eat?* (New York: Hachette Book Group, 2018).

38. Environmental Working Group (EWG) Science Team: EWG 2020 Shopper's Guide to Pesticides in Produce™, Environmental Working Group, March 25, 2020, https://www.ewg.org/foodnews/dirty-dozen.php.

39. Dr. Jason Fung, *Diabetes Code: Prevent and Reverse Type Diabetes Naturally* (British Columbia: Greystone Books Ltd., 2018).

40. Edward Hallowell, "Overloaded Circuits: Why Smart People Underperform," Harvard Business Review, January 2005.

41. Matthew Killingsworth and Daniel Gilbert, "Wandering Mind Is Not a Happy Mind," The Harvard Gazette, November 11, 2010.

42. Bob Weinhold, "Epigenetics: The Science of Change," Environment Health Perspectives, March 2006, https://www.ncbi.nlm.nih.gov/pmc/articles/PMC1392256/.

43. Sergio Elias Hernandex, Jose Suero, Alfons Barros, Jose Luis Gonzales-More, and Katya Rubia, "Increased Grey Matter

Associated with Long-Term Sahaja Yoga Meditation: A Voxel-Based Morphometry Study," US National Library of Medicine, March 3, 2016, https://www.ncbi.nlm.nih.gov/pmc/articles/PMC4777419/.

44. Rick Hanson, *Rewiring Happiness* (New York: Crown Publishing Group, 2013).

45. Christian Keysers and Valeria Gazzola, "Hebbian Learning and Predictive Mirror Neurons for Actions, Sensations and Emotions," US National Library of Medicine, June 5, 2014: https://www.ncbi.nlm.nih.gov/pmc/articles/PMC4006178/.

46. Mindful Staff, "Jon Kabat-Zinn: Defining Mindfulness," Mindful, January 11, 2017: https://www.mindful.org/jon-kabat-zinn-defining-mindfulness/.

47. David M. Levy and Jacob O. Wobbrock, "Initial Results from a Study of the Effects of Meditation on Multitasking Performance," Association of Computing Machinery, 2016, https://dl.acm.org/doi/10.1145/1979742.1979862.

48. Goyal Madhav and Sonal Singh, et al, "Meditation Programs for Psychological Stress and Well-being: A Systematic Review and Meta-Analysis," US National Library of Medicine, 2013, https://pubmed.ncbi.nlm.nih.gov/24395196/.

49. Cortland Dahl, Antonie Lutz, and Richard Davidson," Reconstructing and Deconstructing the Self: Cognitive Mechanisms in Meditation Practice," US National Library of Medicine, July 28, 2015, https://pubmed.ncbi.nlm.nih.gov/26231761/.

50. Fadel Zeidan, Katherine Martucci, and Robert Kraft, et al, "Brain Mechanisms Supporting the Modulation of Pain by Mindfulness Meditation," US National Library of Medicine, April 2, 2011, https://www.ncbi.nlm.nih.gov/pmc/articles/PMC3090218/.

51. Marcia Kiyomi Koike and Roberto Cardoso, "Meditation Can Produce Beneficial Effects to Prevent Cardiovascular Disease," US National Library of Medicine, June 2014, https://pubmed. ncbi.nlm.nih.gov/25390009/.

52. Benjamin Baddeley, "Sitting Is the New Smoking: Where Do We Stand?, *British Journal of General Practice*, May 2016, https://www.ncbi.nlm.nih.gov/pmc/articles/PMC4838429/.

53. Bradberry, Travis and Greaves, Jean, *Emotional Intelligence 2.0* (San Diego: Talent Smart, 2009).

54. Prakhar Verma, "Destroy Negativity From Your Mind With This Simple Exercise," Mission Originals, https://medium.com/the-mission/a-practical-hack-to-combat-negative-thoughts-in-2-minutes-or-less-cc3d1bddb3af

55. Eckart Tolle, *Power of Now* (Vancouver: Namaste Publishing, 1999).

56. Rick Hanson, "Grow Inner Strengths," Just One Thing Blog, 2020.

57. Rollin McCraty, Mike Atkinson, William Tiller, Glenn Rein, and Alan Watkins, "The Effects of Emotions on Short-Term Power Spectrum Analysis of Heart Rate Variability" *The American Journal of Cardiology, vol. 76, no. 14* (November 15, 1995), 1089–93.

58. Ali M Alshami, "Pain: Is It in the Brain or the Heart?," National Library of Medicine, November 14, 2019, https://pubmed. ncbi.nlm.nih.gov/31728781/

59. T. B. Kashdan and Julian T. Uswatte, "Gratitude and Hedonic and Eudaimonic Well-being in Vietnam War Veterans," US National Library of Medicine, February 2006, https:// pubmed.ncbi.nlm.nih.gov/16389060/.

60. Alex Wood, Stephen Joseph, Joanna Lloyd, and Samuel Atkins, "Gratitude Influences Sleep through Mechanism of Pre-Sleep Cognitions," US National Library of Medicine, November 22, 2008, https://pubmed.ncbi.nlm.nih.gov/19073292/.

61. Prathik Kini, Joel Wong, Sydney McInnis, Nicole Gabana, and Joshua Brown, "The Effects of Gratitude Expression on Neural Activity," US National Library of Medicine, December 30, 2015, https://pubmed.ncbi.nlm.nih.gov/26746580/.

62. John Mark Taylor, "Mirror Neurons After a Quarter Century: New Light, New Cracks," Harvard University, July 25, 2016, http://sitn.hms.harvard.edu/flash/2016/mirror-neurons-quarter-century-new-light-new-cracks/

63. Brene Brown, *Daring Greatly: How the Courage to Be Vulnerable Transforms the Way We Live, Love, Parent, and Lead* (New York: Penguin Random House, 2012).

64. Guido Alessandri, Enrico Perinelli, Evelina De Longis, Valentian Rosa, Annalisa Theodorou, and Laura Borgoni, "The Costly Burden of an Inauthentic Self: Insecure Self-Esteem Predisposes to Emotional Exhaustion by Increasing Reactivity to Negative Events," US National Library of Medicine, November 30, 2016, https://pubmed.ncbi.nlm.nih.gov/27852105/.

65. Brene Brown, *Daring Greatly: How the Courage to Be Vulnerable Transforms the Way We Live, Love, Parent, and Lead* (New York: Penguin Random House, 2012).

66. Steven Covey, *The 7 Habits of Highly Effective People* (New York: Simon & Schuster, 1989).

67. Joesph Luciani, "Why 80 Percent of New Year's Resolutions Fail," *U.S. News*, Dec 29, 2015, https://health.usnews.com/health-news/blogs/eat-run/articles/2015-12-29/why-80-percent-of-new-years-resolutions-fail.

NOTES | 175

68. Phillippa Lally, Corelia Jaarveld, Henry Potts, and Jane Wardle, "How Are Habits Formed: Modeling Habit Formation in the Real World," Wiley Online Library, July 16, 2009, https://onlinelibrary.wiley.com/doi/abs/10.1002/ejsp.674.
69. James Clear, *Atomic Habits: An Easy & Proven Way to Build Good Habits & Break Bad Ones* (New York: Penguin Random House, 2018).
70. Elaine Mead, "Comfort Zones: An Alternative Perspective," PyschCentral, November 26, 2018, https://psychcentral.com/blog/comfort-zones-an-alternative-perspective/.
71. Bronnie Ware, *The Top Five Regrets of Dying: A Life Transformed by the Dearly Departing* (New York: Hay House, Inc. August 2012).

Just for You

As a special bonus, I have a free gift for you to relieve stress and build personal resilience. It's a Recharge Your Body starter kit. Go to marymosham.com to sign up for my mailing list. By joining, you will receive monthly articles and information about upcoming events on living your best career and life with success and happiness.

Note to the Reader

Thank you for joining me on this incredible journey. I hope the seven keys and powerful tools for ending burnout and unlocking your greatest potential will be a source of inspiration on your career path. If you've found even a small part of this read beneficial, it would mean a great deal to me if you could leave a review wherever fine books are sold online—and, of course, spread the word!

About the Author

Mary is an award-winning leadership coach, mindfulness teacher, and author. She is dedicated to empowering people to create meaningful careers, lives, and legacies with success, happiness and resilience. With over twenty years of experience in corporate management, change consulting, and leadership development at Fortune 100 companies, she has coached hundreds of top leaders and facilitated workshops around the world.

Mary specializes in leadership, team and personal development, yoga and meditation, and corporate mindfulness. She empowers people to grow their greatest potential, cultivate health and well-being, and make their unique difference in the world. She also partners with organizations to develop high-performing and mindful leaders, teams, and cultures. Trained in neuroscience, psychology, adult development, nutrition, and wisdom traditions over the last two decades, Mary offers practical, evidence-based strategies and powerful tools to achieve break-through results and live your purpose with unshakeable confidence.

Mary has a master's degree in organization development from Pepperdine University and has won numerous awards, including the Cisco Coach Excellence award. She holds certifications in integral and strengths coaching, mindfulness, yoga, emotional intelligence, and Enneagram. She is passionate about traveling, hiking, giving back, and creating a sustainable world.

You can follow Mary on social media and learn about upcoming events at marymosham.com. Explore her transformational coaching and mindfulness solutions to help you create your best career and life with deep fulfillment.